BAD BREAKS ALL AROUND

BAD BREAKS ALL AROUND
THE REPORT OF THE CENTURY FOUNDATION WORKING GROUP ON TAX EXPENDITURES

WITH BACKGROUND PAPERS BY ERIC TODER, BERNARD WASOW, AND MICHAEL P. ETTLINGER

THE CENTURY FOUNDATION PRESS • NEW YORK

The Century Foundation sponsors and supervises timely analyses of economic policy, foreign affairs, and domestic political issues. Not-for-profit and nonpartisan, it was founded in 1919 and endowed by Edward A. Filene.

LIBRARY OF CONGRESS CATALOGING-IN-PUBLICATION DATA

Bad breaks all around : the report of the Century Foundation Working Group on Tax Expenditures / by The Century Foundation.
    p. cm
  Includes bibliographical references and index.
  ISBN 0-87078-464-1 (pbk. : alk. paper)
    1.Tax expenditures—United States. 2.Tax expenditures—Law and legislation—United States. 3.Tax incentives—United States. 4.Government spending policy—United States. I. Century Foundation. Working Group on Tax Breaks.
  HJ4653.T22 B33 2001
  336.2'06—dc21

                                                        2001006985

Manufactured in the United States of America.

FOREWORD

The attacks that began September 11, 2001, at least in the short run, have made all other problems appear trivial. Homeland security, the war against terrorism, and the struggle against economic recession have quite properly dominated public discussion. But as we fight to restore security, life goes on. We may not have politics as usual, but as usual, we have politics.

Contained in the first set of measures Congress addressed after the attacks were several economic programs. The first of these aimed at subsidizing the airline industry, which was threatened with mass bankruptcies. The second was a "stimulus package," ostensibly aimed at injecting new demand into the sagging economy. By accelerating tax reductions for high-income households and retroactively eliminating the alternative minimum tax for corporations, the versions of the stimulus package passed by the House would be "an early Christmas card" for "already profitable corporations," according to Representative Greg Ganske (R-Iowa). The stimulus package favored by the president was not very different, providing enormous benefits to large corporate donors and little to low- and moderate-income households that might actually spend most of their tax cuts. Whether through accelerated deprecation, increased deductibility of business entertainment expenses, or retroactive removal of minimum tax provisions, advocates of these stimulus packages sought to deliver a bouquet of new and expanded tax breaks to their supporters.

If we look back before September 11, the politics of taxation were not much different. The tax bill of spring 2001 provides an excellent example of how pervasive tax breaks are in new and existing tax law in ordinary times. Indeed, the 2001 bill included $275 billion of special tax breaks such as expansion of tax benefits for pension plans and individual retirement accounts (IRAs) and enactment of a new deduction for qualified higher education expenses. The president actually proposed many more tax breaks than were adopted by Congress—$475 billion worth. Among the thirty new and expanded tax breaks the president proposed were such measures as a permanent extension of the research and experimentation (R&E) credit as well as a number of tax breaks aimed at health care and health insurance. The president's energy plan, which closely followed his victory on taxes and was passed by the House of Representatives in August 2001, was essentially another round of special tax breaks—$34 billion worth.

Political manipulation of tax breaks is not a partisan matter. During the 2000 presidential campaign, for example, then-Vice President Gore proposed more than twenty new tax credits for various social and economic purposes.

The reliance on tax breaks poses a clear threat to good government. Consider this: Faced with almost universal hostility to the complexity and perceived favoritism within the tax system, the president and Congress are adding tax breaks every year that make the system *more* difficult to understand and increasingly unequal. Faced with demands for transparency and accountability, elected officials are making it harder and harder to follow how public money is spent. Faced with concern over those left behind in our complex economy, legislators still rely on stealth spending through tax breaks, even though this implicitly excludes the bottom quarter of the population, those who do not earn enough to benefit from most breaks. Faced with a tax system that *they* are making harder and harder to administer, politicians cut back resources of the Internal Revenue Service (IRS) and then joined the chorus of abuse of that agency. No wonder voters are angry at government.

Tax reform will continue to be a critical issue. It is increasingly clear that the brief era of big government surpluses is over and that budget deficits again will dominate the fiscal landscape. It also is very likely that proposals for sweeping reform—replacement of the progressive income tax by a consumption, sales, or a flat tax—will be part of the debate. The prospect for such discussions creates an opportunity for those who would like to see a reduction of special tax breaks, broadening of the tax base, and fundamental simplification of tax rules within the framework of the progressive income tax. We may be approaching one of the rare moments when real tax reform is politically possible. It is important that, as reform takes shape, reasonable voices are not drowned out by special interests.

In the emerging debate about tax reform, The Century Foundation Working Group on Tax Expenditures offers thoughtful and detailed suggestions. The bipartisan Working Group was established during the 2000 election cycle, when it was clear that both major presidential candidates shared the previous administration's fondness for tax breaks. It is composed of experts with a wide range of experience in tax matters. The report argues that tax breaks are a far more important part both of policy and of the politics of tax law than most people realize. While it emphasizes that some tax breaks unquestionably advance worthy goals for American society, the group unanimously agrees that the proliferation of credits, exemptions, and deductions over the past fifteen years is a troublesome trend. Instead of adding new breaks, Congress should weed out, streamline, and subject to ongoing scrutiny the concessions that already exist. The report includes a number of specific ideas for accomplishing that goal, and it highlights some of the most unjustifiable tax breaks.

In this volume, we offer not only the report of the Working Group but also three background papers that informed the group's deliberations. Those papers offer a wealth of analytical and factual insights about "tax expenditures." Eric Toder's paper provides evidence on the growing importance of tax breaks as a policy tool and discusses the problems this raises as well as the circumstances under which the tax code may be a useful vehicle for providing benefits. Bernard Wasow's paper suggests that it is very hard to demonstrate, with evidence or with theory, that tax breaks have the desirable effects on behavior that advocates take for granted. The third is the thorough review of tax breaks by Michael Ettlinger. Bringing up to date and expanding the Citizens for Tax Justice's 1996 publication "The Hidden Entitlements," Ettlinger provides detailed information on the myriad tax breaks to businesses and households as well as careful assessments of the beneficiaries of tax breaks. Not surprisingly, the great majority favor those who already have income and power. The important exception to this generalization is the earned income tax credit, which surely proves the rule that tax breaks make for bad policy and underlines the fact that reform must be careful and selective. For anyone seriously committed to rolling up their sleeves and crafting a comprehensive reform of tax breaks, this volume should provide an invaluable resource.

The members of the Working Group do not agree about everything government should do. Yet, they have reached consensus that the proliferation of tax breaks is undermining not only good government but also public faith in the institution of government. Most of the members of the group have at one time or another been part of government, and they have seen up close what they are criticizing.

The Century Foundation hopes that this report and the background papers that guided the group's deliberations will help raise public awareness about taxation, especially the frequently unfair and often costly consequences of an important and growing problem—the explosion of tax breaks.

Richard C. Leone, *President*
The Century Foundation
May 2002

CONTENTS

LIST OF BOXES AND TABLES

MEMBERS OF THE WORKING GROUP

Donald C. Alexander
Partner, Akin, Gump, Strauss, Hauer & Feld, L.L.P

Jane G. Gravelle
Senior Specialist in Economic Policy, Government and Finance Division, Congressional Research Service

Iris J. Lav
Deputy Director, Center on Budget and Policy Priorities

Robert S. MacIntyre
Director, Citizens for Tax Justice

Leslie B. Samuels
Partner, Cleary, Gottlieb, Steen & Hamilton

John Karl Scholz
Professor of Economics and Director of the Institute for Research on Poverty, University of Wisconsin—Madison

David Smith
Director, Public Policy Department of AFL-CIO

Note: The organizations and affiliations of working group members are listed for the purposes of identification only. The opinions expressed in this report are solely those of the individual working group members.

REPORT OF THE WORKING GROUP

In 2001, for the first time in twenty years, Congress enacted major tax reductions. In addition to income tax rate cuts, elimination of the estate tax, and marriage penalty relief, Congress enacted new and expanded tax breaks amounting to about $275 billion over the next ten years. These included doubling the child credit and making more of it refundable, expanding tax benefits for pension plans and IRAs, and expanding tax incentives for education, in particular, enactment of a new deduction for qualified higher education expenses. Congress did not, however, enact all the tax breaks that the president proposed in his budget, so we can expect some of these to show up in future legislation. Overall, the president proposed more than thirty new and expanded tax breaks costing $475 billion over the next decade. The tax bill did not embrace proposals such as a new refundable tax credit for health insurance, permanent extension of the research and experimentation (R&E) credit, extension of the deduction for charitable contributions to taxpayers who do not itemize deductions, and a new deduction for the purchase of long-term care insurance. The president also proposed new tax incentives for energy production and conservation as part of his energy plan.

Why will such programs as health, education, child care, and energy production and conservation be paid for on the tax side of the budget rather than through direct expenditures? The answer is that special tax breaks allow the president and Congress to spend while appearing to be cutting taxes. The members of The Century Foundation Working Group on Tax Expenditures are concerned about this trend toward using the tax system to undertake disguised spending. It did not start with President Bush: Democrats as well as Republicans are skilled practitioners. In the recent presidential campaign, for example, Vice President Gore proposed more than twenty new tax credits for various social and economic purposes. Such stealth spending makes for bad tax policy as well as inefficient spending. This report is meant to alert the American public to this practice and call for reform.

The federal individual and corporate income taxes currently supply about 60 percent of the revenues needed to fund federal programs. They are progressive in the sense that they take a larger share of the income of high-income than of low-income families. Indeed, income taxes are the main sources of progressivity in the nation's tax system; they offset the regressive effects of other large revenue sources such as payroll taxes (32 percent of federal receipts), federal excise taxes, and state and local sales taxes. Without income taxes, our ability to support adequate funding for national defense, public infrastructure, and a social safety net would be seriously compromised, and a much larger share of the tax burden would be shifted to low- and middle-income families.

Yet the federal income tax and the agency that enforces it, the Internal Revenue Service, have become increasingly unpopular over the past few decades. The income tax, though still progressive, has become riddled with special benefits. Some of these benefits promote good causes, and some, such as the earned income tax credit, arguably belong in the tax code. But many tax benefits are difficult to justify, and the trend toward expanding them has accelerated in recent years. Since 1990, Congress has:

- introduced new tax credits for undergraduate tuition and lifetime learning and a new deduction for higher education expenses;

- expanded eligibility for participation in tax-preferred individual retirement accounts (IRAs), introduced a new, back-loaded IRA (the Roth IRA), and increased IRA contribution limits;

- introduced numerous new, special purpose saving incentives, such as medical savings accounts, education saving accounts, and preferential treatment of prepaid college tuition plans;

- introduced new, targeted incentives for investment and employment in economically disadvantaged areas;

- restored the tax preference for realized capital gains;

- greatly expanded the earned income tax credit, introduced a new child credit, and then increased it; and

- enacted many other tax incentives.

Regardless of the merit of any of the particular special benefits, the aggregate result is a highly complex system that imposes large compliance costs on taxpayers and makes enforcement more difficult, even as enforcement resources for the IRS are constrained. Special tax benefits increase resentment among those who do not qualify for them and endanger the voluntary compliance upon which the system depends. They also impose costs on the economy by diverting resources toward activities favored by the tax system at the expense of other activities that may be more productive. Of course, some subsidies on the spending side of the budget also lack economic justification. But, inserting subsidies into the tax code can make them even more costly than they would otherwise be.

The 1986 Tax Reform Act was a major effort to reverse the trend toward more use of tax breaks. It eliminated a number of individual and corporate tax breaks in exchange for a significant cut in marginal tax rates. However, since 1986 the accretion of tax breaks has resumed. Politicians have looked increasingly to tax breaks as a way of enacting new programs for favored causes and constituencies without having to increase federal spending explicitly (see Box 1, page 6).

One response to the growing complexity of the income tax has been calls to eliminate the individual and corporate income taxes entirely, replacing them with a regressive national consumption tax. Proposals in recent years have focused primarily on either the so-called flat tax, collected in part from wage earners, or a value-added or retail sales tax, collected exclusively from businesses. A second response is simply to heap abuse on the IRS and the tax code generally, without offering constructive solutions.

We believe there is a better way. The key element in tax reform must be a thorough reexamination of existing tax breaks that would lead to elimination of many of them. Such reform is fully compatible with maintaining a progressive income tax as a major component of our revenue system while providing needed tax simplification. It is fully compatible with reducing the level of tax collections to return some of an anticipated budget surplus to the public, as in the recent tax bill. It also is compatible with maintaining or increasing collections to support

---

BOX 1
SPENDING OR TAXES?

Some tax breaks are especially thinly disguised spending programs. An example is the provision in the tax code for Qualified Zone Academy Bonds (QZABs), which subsidize the construction of schools in certain low-income communities. The Department of Education administers the program and allocates a budgeted amount of resources among eligible communities. But, instead of receiving direct interest subsidies, investors in these bonds are awarded certificates that they can use to claim credits against their federal income tax. The credits are exactly equal to the interest costs of the bonds.

Because QZABs are designed like a spending program, they avoid some of the bad features of traditional tax-exempt bonds. They do not create a source of tax-free income for high-income investors and do not make the tax law less progressive if one (correctly) views the tax credits as a substitute for interest income investors would otherwise receive. The question is, however, given that the program is really no different from spending, why is it in the tax code in the first place?

---

existing or expanded funding of social programs, defense, or homeland security, or setting aside more resources to pay for the retirement of the baby boomers.

Limiting tax breaks will be difficult. But, spending less on tax expenditures makes it easier to keep rates low and to provide additional relief for low- and middle-income families. Restraining spending hidden through the tax code serves the goals of both those who want government programs to be more effective and those who favor a smaller and less intrusive government.

WHAT IS A TAX BREAK?

By tax break, we have in mind a provision that offers special or preferential benefits to selected taxpayers or for selected economic activities. Some people use the term *tax expenditure* as another name for these special provisions. The term suggests that these tax breaks should be considered a form of spending in disguise. Tax breaks resemble spending because they are a government-directed use of economic resources, which ultimately must be paid for by imposing higher general taxes on the population or by reducing other forms of spending.

The Office of Management and Budget (OMB) and the congressional Joint Committee on Taxation (JCT) annually publish lists of tax expenditures and estimates of their budgetary effects. These agencies define tax expenditures as "special exclusions, exemptions, deductions, credits, or tax rates." The key word in this definition is *special;* lower tax rates based on a broad criterion such as a taxpayer's income are not a "tax expenditure," but selectively lower rates for narrow groups of taxpayers or activities are tax expenditures. Obviously, the definition of either a "tax expenditure" or "tax break" presumes that there is some baseline income tax system against which certain provisions are "special" or exceptions (see Box 2).

Box 2
DARK CLOUDS?

The opening paragraph of the Analytical Perspectives section of the 2002 federal budget questions the value of tax expenditure data:

> Underlying the "tax expenditure" concept is the notion that the Federal government would otherwise collect additional revenues but for these provisions. It assumes an arbitrary tax base is available to the Government in its entirety as a resource to be spent. Because of the breadth of this arbitrary tax base, the Administration believes that the concept of "tax expenditure" is of questionable analytic value. The discussion below is based on material and formats developed and included in previous budgets. The Administration intends to reconsider this presentation in the future.

The Working Group welcomes periodic review of the conceptual foundation of "tax expenditures," but we think that historically comparable data on this important feature of our tax system are essential for good policymaking. It would be a serious mistake to stop publishing tax expenditure numbers just because they are controversial. We need more information to guide policymaking, not less.

The baseline system used by both OMB and JCT to measure tax expenditures is an income tax system that allows for graduated rates for individuals, different treatment of married couples and single individuals, and adjustments for family size. Some analysts might prefer using other baselines for defining a tax break.[1]

The Working Group recognizes that identification and measurement of some tax breaks are controversial. But most tax expenditures on the OMB/JCT lists would be counted as tax breaks under any reasonable definition. And, most of the new tax credits and deductions that politicians are proposing would be tax breaks under almost anyone's definition.

THE USE OF TAX EXPENDITURES IS GROWING, WITH BIPARTISAN SUPPORT

In recent years, tax expenditures have become an important way to conduct social and economic policy without the appearance of spending money. The past decade has seen enactment of many new tax breaks and expansion of existing ones:

- The preferential treatment of capital gains realized by individuals, eliminated in the 1986 Tax Reform Act, has been restored. The top rate on long-term gains was reduced to 20 percent in 1997. The revenue loss from this preference will be $41.8 billion in fiscal year 2001.

- In 1997, Congress enacted several new tax credits and exclusions for expenses of postsecondary education. The new credits will cost $6.3 billion in 2001. A new deduction for higher education expenses, enacted in May 2001, will cost about $10 billion over the next five years.

- Congress has made tax incentives for retirement saving more generous by expanding eligibility for individual retirement accounts (IRAs), enacting a new, nondeductible IRA (the Roth IRA), and liberalizing rules for salary reduction plans. The cost of retirement saving incentives increased from $60.3 billion in 1990 to $114.3 billion in 2001 and will increase further as investors benefit from the tax-free interest on Roth IRAs. New incentives enacted in May 2001 will cost an additional $50 billion over the next ten years.

* In 1990 and 1993, Congress enacted large increases in the earned income tax credit (EITC), which were phased in over several years. The annual cost of the EITC increased from $5.5 billion in 1990 to $30.6 billion in 2001. Marriage penalty relief and other provisions enacted in 2001 will add an additional $2.3 billion per year to the cost of the EITC by the end of this decade.

* Since 1993, Congress has enacted numerous new and narrowly targeted tax incentives, including those that support investment in economically disadvantaged communities, investment in environmental remediation expenses, employment of former welfare recipients, and a host of other activities.

The last Clinton administration budget proposed a mass of new and expanded tax expenditures. Those included new tax credits for retirement saving accounts and long-term care expenses and increases in the lifetime learning credit, for postsecondary school tuition, the earned income tax credit, and the dependent care credit. President Bush also proposed a wide variety of new tax incentives in his first budget (see Box 3, pages 10 and 11).[2] Some, but not all, of these proposals were enacted in May 2001.

Many new tax expenditures also originate in Congress. In the past year, the following incentives, among others, were actively considered by Congress: expanded IRAs and increased pension contribution limits, additional deductions for health insurance, increased business meal deductions, increased expensing limits for small-business equipment investments, and education savings accounts. While Congress in this year's tax bill did not enact all of the tax breaks proposed by the president in the budget, it introduced some new tax expenditures that were absent in the budget and expanded other proposals. New tax benefits not in the president's budget included increases in the IRA contributions limits, a new deduction for higher education expenses, and increases in the dependent care credit.

Box 3
Tax Breaks in the President's Budget

The president's 2002 budget proposals featured a large number of new and expanded tax breaks. The tax breaks that President Bush proposed would have cost about $475 billion over the next ten years.

The president's budget included proposals to:

- increase the child credit;

- provide a refundable tax credit for the purchase of health insurance to individuals and families who do not receive employer-sponsored health insurance and do not qualify for public programs;

- introduce an above-the-line deduction for charitable contributions;

- make the research and experimentation credit permanent;

- provide an above-the-line deduction for long-term care insurance expenses;

- provide a tax credit for developers of affordable single-family housing;

- allow up to $500 in unused benefits in "health flexible spending accounts" to be carried forward to the next year;

- increase and expand educational savings accounts;

- provide an additional personal exemption to caretakers of elderly family members;

- extend permanently and expand medical savings accounts;

- extend permanently the expensing of certain environmental remediation costs ("brownfields");

- provide teachers an above-the-line deduction of up to $400 per year for out-of-pocket classroom expenses;

BOX 3 CONTINUED
TAX BREAKS IN THE PRESIDENT'S BUDGET

- permit tax-free and penalty-free withdrawals from individual retirement accounts (IRAs) for charitable purposes;

- increase and make permanent the adoption tax credit;

- raise the cap on corporate charitable contributions;

- provide a 50 percent capital gains exclusion on the sale of land or an interest in land or water for conservation purposes;

- modify treatment of nuclear decommissioning costs;

- establish individual development accounts;

- extend subpart-F exceptions to active financial sector income;

- exampt all qualified prepaid tuition and savings plans from tax and extend coverage to independent (private prepaid tution plans);

- establish Farm, Fish, and Ranch Risk Management (FFARRM) savings accounts; and

- provide other tax benefits

WHY TAX EXPENDITURES ARE A CONCERN

The Working Group recognizes that some tax breaks promote worthwhile objectives and does not propose indiscriminate elimination of all such incentives. But, we are deeply concerned about the growing tendency to funnel more and more social and economic policy through the tax code. The growth in tax breaks imposes costs on the economy and erodes confidence in the progressive income tax. It conceals the growth in government intervention in the economy by making new programs look like tax cuts. Moreover, in most cases, direct spending programs could accomplish more effectively the goals that tax incentives are meant to advance.

TAX EXPENDITURES IMPOSE COSTS ON THE ECONOMY, TAXPAYERS, AND THE IRS

Tax breaks in many cases impose costs on the economy. They interfere with market incentives, channeling resources toward tax-favored activities at the expense of others with higher returns. They make the tax laws much more complex, requiring numerous fine distinctions between those activities or taxpayers that do or do not qualify for benefits. This complexity raises compliance costs for both individual and business taxpayers and makes it more difficult and costly for the IRS to administer the law. Even when taxpayers can reduce these problems by using tax software, the multiplicity of special provisions makes it much harder for them to understand how their tax liability is calculated.

TAX EXPENDITURES MAKE THE INCOME TAX LESS FAIR AND ERODE ITS CREDIBILITY

Tax breaks allow some people to pay much less tax than others with the same income. This favorable treatment of some taxpayers fosters resentment not only among those who cannot use the breaks but also among some who object to the complexity even as they use tax incentives. Taxpayer frustration and resentment endanger the voluntary compliance upon which tax administration depends.

SOME TAX EXPENDITURES PROMOTE IMPORTANT SOCIAL GOALS BUT THEY ARE OFTEN LESS EFFICIENT THAN DIRECT SPENDING

Many tax breaks serve important social and economic goals. The earned income tax credit lifts the income of many working families above the poverty line and eases the transition from welfare to work. Other incentives encourage employers to provide health care for their workers and to support charitable giving. Tax incentives account for a significant share of federal support for health care for the nonelderly, housing, and saving for retirement.

But often tax incentives are inferior substitutes for direct spending. The political climate encourages the use of the tax system to fund new programs because the public has accepted the notion that spending is "bad" and tax cuts are "good." New tax breaks allow politicians to have their cake and eat it too—providing new programs and special benefits for favored constituencies while appearing to support a smaller and less intrusive government.

This political bias toward using the tax system has two bad effects. First, many proposals that would not be taken seriously if presented as new spending can be enacted if disguised as tax cuts. For example, it is hard to imagine that Congress would have enacted a direct outlay that paid 75 percent of the first $2,000 of tuition costs for college students from families with incomes from about $25,000 up to $100,000 a year while completely denying benefits to families with two or more children and income less than $25,000 (who pay no income tax) and providing reduced benefits to families with two children and incomes between $25,000 and about $34,000 (who pay very little income tax). But this subsidy schedule is precisely what the HOPE scholarship tax credit offers.

Second, even for some proposals that would pass muster as a direct outlay, the tax code is often a poor subsidy vehicle. For example, in contrast to spending programs, most tax expenditures by design provide no help to the lowest-income families and to unprofitable businesses. Beyond the exclusion of the lowest-income families, those tax breaks that work by reducing taxable income—either through an extra deduction or exemption or an acceleration of deductions—also subsidize some taxpayers more than others. This additional subsidy occurs because deductions and exemptions are worth more to those in the highest marginal tax brackets than to the majority of taxpayers, who are in the 15 percent rate bracket.

Even if a program is well structured, the IRS is not normally the right agency to administer resources that require programmatic expertise to determine where they should go. Making the IRS responsible adds more complexity and administrative burdens to the system (see Box 4, page 14).

That being said, we recognize that Congress is not about to call a halt to all use of the tax code to promote social and economic goals. This recognition requires us to ask the following questions:

- What principles should determine when to provide a tax break?

- When is it better for a tax break to be recast as direct spending?

- If tax expenditures are to be used, how should they be designed?

STANDARDS FOR EVALUATING TAX BREAKS

Four main questions should be considered in evaluating existing tax breaks and proposed new ones. First, is there a need for any government intervention at all, and is the existing or proposed intervention effective? Why not let the market handle it and use the revenue lost on the tax break for other spending or broader tax cuts?

Second, assuming an existing tax break fails on the first criterion, would there be major economic disruption from eliminating it? If so, are there ways to minimize the disruption?

Third, even if a program is justified, is it best implemented through a tax break or would it be more effective and transparent to have a direct spending program instead?

Fourth, assuming there ought to be a tax break, are some ways of designing it better than others?

Box 4
Tuition Credits and Pell Grants

In 1997 Congress enacted two major new tax incentives for postsecondary education—the HOPE scholarship credit and the lifetime learning credit. The HOPE scholarship credit helps students and families pay tuition costs for the first two years of undergraduate education. The lifetime learning credit is less generous than the HOPE scholarship credit but supports college education beyond the first two years, graduate education, and education and training later in life. These credits help middle-income families but, because they are not refundable, do not benefit families at the lowest income levels who most need assistance. Students from poor families, however, receive assistance from Pell Grants, a program on the spending side of the budget. An alternative to the tuition tax credits would have been to expand Pell Grants to provide more assistance to middle-income families. Use of the Pell Grant program for this new subsidy would have utilized an existing administrative mechanism and would have avoided many problems encountered in designing programs as tax incentives administered by the IRS. But expanding Pell Grants to the middle class would have made the nature of the subsidy more transparent, and that might have made it more difficult politically to enact.

Is There a Need for Government Intervention?

The basic premise of our economic system is that freely competitive markets will usually lead businesses to produce the goods most valued by consumers in the least costly ways and to invest in capital goods and new technologies that yield the highest prospective returns. To justify a tax break (or new spending program) that subsidizes some activities at the expense of others, one must ask why this market process produces too little of the preferred good or inadequate investment in the favored investment or technology. In general, insufficient output or investment will occur only when the benefits to society as a whole from these goods, services, or investments exceed the benefits to providers and purchasers. For example, the benefits of public vaccination programs may exceed the gains to those vaccinated by protecting those not vaccinated from epidemics.

The existence of such market failures for some goods or capital justifies their public provision or subsidy. Examples include police protection, maintenance of air and water quality, and basic public education. But for most goods and services that people value—such as clothing, automobiles, and vacation travel—and arguably for others—such as housing and higher education for the nonpoor—private markets perform quite well in generating substantial output at the lowest production cost. Similarly, most business decisions—what to produce, how to produce it, and where to invest—are just what the economy needs. Market failure can be said to occur only when there is a compelling case that the free market produces too little of some activities and, by implication, too much of competing activities.

It is not as though tax incentives can increase the production of housing, petroleum, or timber without cost. In making some activities more attractive, subsidies draw resources away from alternative uses. If those alternative uses have more value than the subsidized activity, the total economic welfare of society is reduced. For example, the tax shelters of the early 1980s contributed to excess construction of commercial structures. Some so-called see-through office buildings went for a considerable period without tenants.

The Working Group believes that, other than provisions specifically designed to help low-income families, tax expenditures should be provided only if there is clearly a market failure. We recognize that not everyone will agree when a market failure is present and that the political system will ultimately determine what types of governmental intervention the public favors. But, we strongly believe that proponents of tax breaks should be required to explain what market failure the tax break is trying to correct. This criterion alone would expose the hollow justifications for many existing tax breaks—including those that favor certain forms of energy use (oil and gas, alcohol fuels), those that promote exports by some corporations, and those that favor some forms of capital investment (machinery and equipment) over others. Further, it would highlight how some widely used tax breaks—such as the mortgage interest deduction or tax credits for higher education expenses—also have weak justifications.

The existence of a market failure that needs correction only establishes the possibility that a tax break may be useful. The Working Group believes several other tests are very important in evaluating tax breaks:

- Assuming that market failure leads to too little of some productive activity, a tax break should be cost-effective in the sense that it generates a large enough increase in the desired activity to justify the revenue loss. The tax break should not merely pay for investment and consumption that would occur even without the tax benefit; it should stimulate significant additional activity. For example, one can argue that markets do not produce enough basic scientific research because those who discover new products or techniques often cannot fully capture the value the new ideas generate for others who use them. But a tax credit for business research and experimentation (R&E) is worth doing only if it increases the social value of research firms by an amount that justifies its cost.

- Tax breaks should be appropriately targeted, although proper targeting is often difficult to accomplish. They should be narrow enough to apply only to the activity that requires subsidy (or people that merit assistance), but not so narrow that they overly limit the methods of achieving their goals. For example, the tax exemption of interest on state and municipal bonds provides a subsidy for state and local spending, but the subsidy is arguably both too broad and too narrow. It is too broad because it applies to all state and local activities, not just those that produce national benefits (for which a subsidy may be justified). But it is too narrow because it applies only to costs of capital, thereby encouraging states and localities to substitute capital for labor in production.

- Tax breaks should not unduly compromise the progressivity of the income tax. The benefits of many existing tax breaks go mostly to upper-income families.[3] Examples are the preferences for capital gains, tax-exempt securities, and accelerated depreciation of certain business investments. We are not suggesting that every single item in the tax law be subject to a burden distribution test. Some business tax breaks (for example, the R&E credit) may be justified on economic grounds. But the distribution of tax burdens is important to people's perception of the fairness of the tax system. It may be possible to combine regressive tax expenditures with other changes in the tax law to preserve overall progressivity, but the more the tax base is whittled away by tax expenditures, the higher the rates must be on what remains. Thus, an important benefit of reducing tax breaks is that it permits a lowering of rates without sacrificing revenue or making the tax law less progressive.

- Whatever their other benefits may be, tax breaks should not add excessively to the complexity of the income tax. The Working Group recognizes that there are trade-offs among goals, and some additional complexity may be worth paying for provisions that produce real economic benefits. But, many tax expenditures create considerable complexity without offsetting benefits to efficiency or fairness. An example that troubles the Working Group members is the complicated and overlapping set of retirement saving incentives (deductible IRAs, Roth IRAs, 401(k) plans, SIMPLE plans, SEP plans, education saving accounts, medical saving accounts) and the intricate and varying qualifying rules for such plans. Another troubling example is the complex set of rules for determining the preferential rates on capital gains.

Complex provisions that benefit a minority of taxpayers create an environment where people believe that others who are smarter, better connected, or less scrupulous are getting away with not paying their fair share. This perception undermines voluntary compliance, which is the bedrock of our tax system.[4]

POTENTIAL FOR ECONOMIC DISRUPTION

Before repealing existing tax expenditures, potential economic disruptions must be considered, even for provisions that could not be justified if the tax law were being designed from scratch. Families make economic decisions in the expectation that long-standing tax expenditures will continue. Precipitous removal of the home mortgage interest deduction, for example, could cause the price of houses to decline. The Working Group recognizes the political difficulties and concerns about fairness that removing some widely used tax breaks millions of people rely on would produce. Nonetheless, even broadly popular tax breaks can be gradually whittled away over time. For example, Congress has placed a ceiling on the size of mortgage eligible for an interest deduction (admittedly a very high one of $1 million) and has limited the deduction for home equity loans to interest on $100,000 of borrowing.

While conceptually similar transition concerns apply, we are much less concerned about the disruptive effect of removing narrowly targeted incentives that lack either a strong economic rationale or a broad constituency. Such incentives include existing tax subsidies for natural resource extraction (oil and gas, minerals, and timber), deposits in selected financial institutions (credit unions), promotion of exports, and benefits for selected activities (airports, ports, sports stadiums) financed with tax-exempt bonds. Narrowly targeted incentives can be eliminated or phased out, with appropriate transition relief, in the same way that many similar incentives were wiped off the books in the 1982, 1984, and 1986 tax acts.

It is most important to resist creating new and unjustifiable tax breaks, especially big ones. Once any provision gets into the tax law and consolidates a constituency, it becomes that much harder to remove.

WHY NOT A DIRECT EXPENDITURE?

For any proposed new tax expenditure, policymakers should consider whether its stated objectives might be achieved more effectively through a spending program. In contrast to tax breaks, spending programs are more transparent because their costs are made explicit and their overall contribution to public activity in the economy is apparent. This increased transparency facilitates democratic decisionmaking.

We emphasize that many proposed tax breaks would not receive serious consideration if the identical program design were presented as a spending initiative with payments made by a program agency instead of as tax rebates administered by the IRS. If a program cannot pass muster as new spending, then it should not be enacted as disguised spending through the tax code.

In many cases, direct spending is preferable to tax breaks for additional reasons:

- Some programs require expert review to allocate scarce budgetary resources (grants for scientific research or subsidies to promote the use of energy-efficient technologies). In those cases, it is best to use spending instead of tax credits. The IRS lacks the expertise and institutional culture to perform social services or program evaluations; its job is collecting and refunding taxes. If the IRS must be used, its role is best limited to distributing cash according to specific and readily quantifiable criteria.

- For some programs, the ideal time frame for eligibility assessment or frequency of payment may differ from the annual accounting period of the income tax. Recipients of benefit programs (food stamps, health insurance subsidies) typically need to receive cash benefits more often than annually. Other programs may base payments on a longer period of measurement (for example, Social Security benefits depend on the highest thirty-five years of earnings) and therefore do not fit the annual period for measuring income.

- Where Congress is especially concerned about abuse or fraud, more detailed monitoring by a program agency is preferable to random audits at the relatively low rate (much less than 1 percent) used by the IRS. A congressional directive to raise the audit rate applied to any specific tax break could improve the enforcement of that provision. But singling out one provision for more intensive scrutiny would divert resources from audits that produce more revenue and would lead to complaints about discriminatory enforcement of the tax law.

That being said, the Working Group recognizes that sometimes it is more cost-effective to use the tax system instead of a new spending program to make payments. Tax incentives avoid the need to create a new agency, although they do impose an additional burden on the IRS. A tax break can be a low-cost way to pay benefits when such benefits depend on objectively measured standards (such as the amount of home mortgage interest paid). And, using tax returns lowers costs if eligibility for assistance depends on data that are already reported to the IRS (such as income or number of dependents with Social Security numbers).

The tax system also may have some advantages as a way of delivering benefits that are limited to the working poor. This group, with incomes roughly in the $10,000–$30,000 range, has relatively few programs targeted to it, so there are few existing agencies that might handle the necessary administration on their behalf. Tax benefits also are more "user-friendly" than spending programs because beneficiaries can self-report eligibility on their return instead of applying to a special agency for benefits. Working people who may merit support based on economic need but do not wish to be stigmatized as "welfare recipients" are more likely to claim a tax benefit than participate in a spending program. The flip side of greater participation with a tax break, however, is that there also might be a higher rate of excess claims by those who do not qualify for the benefit.

IF THE TAX SYSTEM MUST BE USED, HOW SHOULD TAX EXPENDITURES BE STRUCTURED?

The Working Group believes that if there are to be explicit subsidies through the tax code, they should generally be designed as credits that provide the same subsidy rate to all taxpayers. Alternative ways to structure tax expenditures—as exemptions, deductions, or exclusions from income—usually are regressive, delivering disproportionate benefits to those in high tax brackets. While deductions are the appropriate way to adjust for differences in ability to pay federal income tax, subsidies to encourage certain activities (such as energy conservation or college tuition) should be in the form of credits (see Box 5).[5]

Even tax credits, however, will not provide the same subsidy to all potential recipients unless they are made refundable—that is, unless taxpayers can receive a net payment from the IRS, not merely an offset to the income taxes they have to pay. Spending programs, such as food stamps (or agricultural subsidies), do not deny benefits to low-income individuals (or unprofitable companies) simply because their earnings (or profits) are low. Yet, a nonrefundable child care or health insurance subsidy that takes the form of a tax break will exclude all households too poor to pay income taxes. Similarly, an R&E credit will not benefit an unprofitable firm, regardless of the social benefits that may flow from its research, unless the credit is refundable or transferable.

If an activity such as child care merits a public subsidy, it is difficult to make the case that the subsidy should be limited to those who pay positive income taxes, excluding low-income families who may need it the most. Yet that is the result of a nonrefundable tax credit.

BOX 5
THE EARNED INCOME TAX CREDIT

The earned income tax credit (EITC) is currently the largest single federal program for poor families. By providing refundable tax credits up to almost $4,000 per year for qualifying working families with children, it has raised the incomes of millions to a level above the poverty line. The Working Group strongly supports the goal of providing cash assistance to low-income working families to encourage their participation in the workforce and to reduce poverty.

In addition to its sound goals, there are other advantages to structuring the EITC as a refundable tax credit: benefits are conditioned on earnings and family size, both already reported in tax returns. Beneficiaries overwhelmingly prefer annual to monthly payouts, again compatible with the tax cycle. Also, a tax rebate appears to be a more user-friendly system than need-based spending programs (welfare). Finally, the working poor targeted by the EITC are relatively easy to reach in this way.

The Working Group recognizes that an earned income tax credit has much greater political marketability than an earnings subsidy administered as a direct expenditure and does not wish to see the program dismantled or cut back. Nevertheless, it is clear that a subsidy for the working poor alternatively could be structured as an expenditure program (with, of course, a new agency to administer the program) rather than as a refundable tax break.

In spite of the case for refundable tax credits, until the 2001 tax bill, virtually no tax break, with the exception of the earned income tax credit and small portion of the child credit was refundable. The 2001 tax act made more of the child credit refundable, thereby expanding its benefits to many low-income working families. The Working Group believes that nonrefundability is a bad way of limiting the fiscal costs of programs because it arbitrarily denies program benefits to those who might be most deserving (and who often pay federal payroll and excise taxes). But we also recognize that adding more refundable credits increases enforcement burdens on the IRS and adds to compliance problems. In short, many existing tax subsidies and new subsidies (such as health insurance tax credits) that proponents want to place in the tax system should be refundable as a matter of program design. But the very need to make these programs refundable is a strong argument for keeping them out of the tax system altogether and placing them on the spending side of the budget.

THE DIRTY DOZEN AND TROUBLESOME TEN

Based on the criteria set forth in this report, the Working Group believes many special allowances in the existing income tax are unjustified. We have selected a "dirty dozen" list of those tax expenditures that we believe should be eliminated (see Box 6). Most of these are narrowly targeted provisions that do not correct for market failures or help disadvantaged groups and could be eliminated or phased out without causing widespread disruption.

We also include a second list, which we label the "troublesome ten" (see Box 7, page 24). Tax expenditures in this group are problematic but have some economic justification.[6] For example, the special tax rates for realized capital gains favor one form of capital income over others (dividends, interest), provide disproportionate benefits to high-income taxpayers, and, in our view, do not stimulate economic growth as their supporters claim. But they also can be defended as correcting (although imperfectly) for the failure to adjust gains for inflation, reducing the burden of the double taxation of corporate income, and mitigating a "lock-in" effect that occurs because the tax is imposed when gains are realized, not when accrued. We list the items in the troublesome ten because they are large in revenue terms and

---

Box 6
The Dirty Dozen

- Export tax incentives (exclusion of income of foreign sales corporations and inventory property sales source rule exception)

- Excess of percentage depletion over cost depletion (fuels and nonfuel minerals)

- Regional economic development incentives (empowerment zones, enterprise communities, and others)

- Graduated corporate income tax rates

- Exemption of interest on private activity state and local bonds (small-issue bonds, energy facility bonds, owner-occupied mortgage subsidy bonds, rental housing bonds, bonds for private, nonprofit educational facilities, hospital construction bonds)

- Tax credits for nonconventional fuels (alternative fuel production credit, alcohol fuel credit) and partial exemption from the motor fuels excise tax for alcohol fuels

- Medical savings accounts

- Exemption of credit union income

- Timber subsidies (expensing of multiperiod timber growing costs, capital gains treatment of certain timber income, and investment credit and seven year amortization for reforestation)

- Special rules for employee stock ownership plans (ESOPs)

- Small life insurance company deduction

- Exclusion of fringe benefits through cafeteria plans

---

therefore merit careful scrutiny. There are good arguments for modifying all of them and eliminating or restructuring many.

BOX 7
THE TROUBLESOME TEN

- Tuition tax incentives (HOPE scholarship, lifetime learning credit, deferral of income on state prepaid tuition programs, education saving bonds)

- Capital gains preferences (preferential tax rates and step-up in basis at death)

- Accelerated depreciation of machinery and equipment

- Credit for low-income housing investment

- Exclusion of contributions and earnings for Individual Retirement Accounts (for individuals with pension coverage)

- Exclusion of interest on public purpose state and local bonds

- Expensing of certain small investments

- Exclusion of interest on life insurance savings

- Exclusion of income earned abroad by U.S. citizens

- Deductibility of state and local property tax on owner-occupied homes

---

CHANGES IN BUDGET PROCESS AND INFORMATION REPORTING

Existing budget rules constrain changes in taxation, discretionary spending, and entitlements. The Working Group considered whether modifications to these budget procedures, aimed especially at tax expenditures, might limit unwarranted expansions of tax concessions. We concluded that supplementing existing budget rules with explicit limitations on tax expenditures was likely to be ineffective and might have harmful side effects. The Working Group believes, however, that more public information could be helpful in increasing awareness of the benefits from eliminating unwarranted tax expenditures and in preventing the enactment of new ones.

LIMITATIONS OF FORMAL BUDGET CONTROLS ON TAX EXPENDITURES

Existing budgetary procedures contain two types of limitations. First, legislated ceilings in past budget acts (the latest in 1997) limit the total amount Congress can spend in any year on discretionary programs. Second, the pay-as-you-go (PAYGO) rules require that any legislated increase in mandatory spending (entitlements) or legislated reduction in tax revenues, relative to the current law baseline, be balanced by an offsetting cut in mandatory spending or increase in taxes. The Working Group believes that these budgetary rules have helped curtail deficits over the past decade and have contributed to the shift in the budget from deficit to surplus. We recognize, however, that Congress in recent years has breached the discretionary caps and that the recent Bush administration-sponsored tax cut ignores the PAYGO rules. We are less optimistic that these controls can be effective in any era of projected budget surpluses.

The PAYGO rules indirectly limit tax expenditures. Under PAYGO, if Congress increases any tax expenditure, it must offset the revenue loss either by reducing other tax expenditures, by increasing taxes, or by cutting mandatory spending. But there are no explicit limitations on aggregate tax expenditures. Congress can increase tax expenditures if it is willing to increase revenues from other tax provisions (by, for example, raising income tax rates, lowering personal exemptions, or increasing tobacco excise taxes) or to reduce mandatory spending (for example, Medicare or Social Security). In the 1997 Budget Act, cuts in Medicare spending and increases in some excise taxes (the aviation trust fund taxes) helped pay for new tax expenditures, such as the child credit and tax credits for costs of postsecondary education. Although tax expenditures did increase in the past decade, in spite of the PAYGO rules, they might have increased much more in the absence of these limits.

We considered possible ways of limiting tax expenditures as a separate category. These techniques included ceilings on total tax expenditures, PAYGO rules applied to tax expenditures alone, combined limits on tax expenditures within defined budget categories (such as energy or housing), ceilings for individual tax expenditures, and mechanisms to reduce tax expenditures automatically if their revenue loss exceeds a preset amount. We also considered increased use of "sunset" rules. We concluded that new budgetary rules applied to tax expenditures were not likely to improve policy outcomes and might make matters worse:

- The measurement of tax expenditures is controversial because it depends on a definition of what a "normal" or baseline tax system looks like. Rules that produce automatic cuts when tax expenditures exceed a specified amount therefore could be viewed as arbitrary and subject to dispute;

- In contrast, the current budgetary rules require much less staff discretion. Staff must estimate revenue effects of tax provisions but need not divide the revenue effect into a "tax expenditure" portion and a "general tax provision" portion;

- Aggregate ceilings on tax expenditures would limit policy choices too much. There is little reason to expect such a ceiling would effectively function to constrain the worst tax expenditures rather than the best.

It could be argued that a PAYGO rule limited to tax expenditures would have a beneficial effect. It is possible that the broader PAYGO rules in effect in the 1990s stopped many small, targeted tax expenditures from becoming law by requiring explicit, offsetting tax increases or entitlement cuts. A PAYGO limited to tax expenditures could make it more difficult to use any savings from future restraint in the growth in entitlement programs from being diverted to new tax expenditures. But, as noted above, any form of limitation on tax expenditures would not sort out good tax expenditures from the bad ones. It could, for instance, lead to cuts in the EITC as the only way to finance new tax expenditures that powerful special interest groups want. In addition, limits that target tax expenditures as a separate category raise all the definitional issues discussed above.

Possible Changes in Reporting

Although the Working Group recommends no changes in budgetary procedures regarding tax breaks, it does believe that more information on tax expenditures would help the legislative process and could make it harder to enact unjustifiable tax breaks. Such additional information on tax expenditures could be routinely produced by government tax analysis agencies, such as the Office of Tax Analysis (OTA) at the U.S. Treasury Department, the Joint Committee on Taxation (JCT), or the Congressional Budget Office (CBO). Any additional information requirement should be accompanied by an increase in the tax analysis agencies' budget and staffing to pay for the additional work.

Types of information that would be desirable include:

- Combined revenue losses for all tax expenditures and tax expenditures by budget function. Such estimates should take account of interactions among separate tax expenditure items. The current tax expenditure budget estimates the cost of each provision as if all the others were fully in effect but does not provide estimates of the total cost of provisions. Adding up the estimates for each item would not provide an accurate measure of the cost of all provisions because eliminating one provision would likely (though not always) change the cost of the remaining ones. For example, if the mortgage interest deduction were repealed, the deductions for state and local income and property taxes would cost less than the figures shown in the tax expenditure budget because fewer people would then itemize deductions on their tax returns. Combining revenue losses from a group of proposals would not be a new exercise; the Treasury and JCT already take account of interactions when estimating the revenue effects of proposed legislation.

- Data on historical trends in tax expenditure totals, using estimating methodologies that are consistent over time.

- Distributional estimates for all tax expenditures as a group and for large, separate tax expenditures that affect the individual income tax. (The Joint Tax Committee periodically does publish estimates of the distributional effects of selected tax expenditures in the individual income tax.)

- Periodic reviews that would cover all tax expenditures over a five-year cycle, with some reviews published in each year. These would provide specific information for each item reviewed. We are not suggesting that the reviews must evaluate the merits of provisions but rather that they furnish information that will enable others to undertake such evaluations. Data on specific provisions might specify, for example:

▲ the number of taxpayers benefiting;

▲ the dollar amount of benefit per taxpayer;

▲ the distribution of benefits among income groups, age groups, or family types;

▲ changes in the use of the tax expenditure over time; and

▲ the amount of the activity being subsidized.

The Working Group recognizes the political incentives and dynamics that encourage the growth of tax breaks. But we believe that the prospect of more information reporting might restrain advocates of some of the more egregious provisions. We also believe that information on the aggregate effects of tax breaks—especially their impact and their effect on the distribution of the tax burden—and on their growth over time would help frame the discussion on the use of the tax system to promote social and economic goals.

Requirements for Better Justification

The Working Group considered whether it might be useful to demand more formal statements justifying new tax breaks when they are proposed by the executive branch and when they are considered by the tax-writing committees of the U.S. House of Representatives and Senate. Such statements might be required to answer the following questions:

• Why is a government program necessary at all? What market failure underlies the need for this tax break?

• What objectives is the tax break meant to accomplish? How would its success or failure be measured?

- What evidence can be cited that suggests the tax break will accomplish these objectives at an acceptable cost? Do most of the tax benefits go for activities that would have been undertaken without the tax break or does it increase the desired activity?

- Why is a tax break better than a direct spending program for accomplishing this purpose?

This exercise is similar to a requirement in an Office of Management Budget (OMB) circular that has been in effect since the 1970s but has fallen into disuse over a period of years, even though it remains official policy.[7]

CONCLUSIONS

Tax expenditures are growing. In the 2000 election campaign, both candidates proposed new tax subsidies to promote social and economic policy goals. Some of these new tax breaks were included in the May 2001 tax cut bill. There will be continuing pressure on the Bush administration to propose, and on Congress to enact, new tax subsidies and expand existing ones.

Although some tax breaks promote useful purposes, their growth overall has harmful effects. Special provisions that promote selected activities or benefit certain categories of taxpayer make the tax law more complicated. By so doing, they make it more costly for taxpayers to comply with the law and for the IRS to administer it. By enabling many people to pay less tax than others with the same income, tax breaks add to the public perception that the tax law is unfair.

Tax breaks obscure the costs and consequences of government spending programs. Programs that would not pass muster as direct spending can be more easily enacted when disguised as tax cuts. Moreover, tax breaks are often less effective than direct spending in accomplishing program goals.

The Century Foundation Working Group on Tax Expenditures encourages the Bush administration and Congress to consider which existing tax breaks can be scaled back or eliminated and to exercise restraint in proposing new ones. Only by simplifying the tax code and cutting out those tax incentives that are no longer justified can we address the popular perception that our tax system is too complex and unfair for most citizens.

Reducing or even restraining the growth of tax breaks is always difficult. Yet, whatever future decisions are made regarding the optimal level of federal taxation overall, paring back preferences in the tax code will make it easier to achieve the fundamental goals of making tax policy simpler, more equitable, and less costly to the economy. With less money spent on tax breaks, there will be more funds available to keep marginal tax rates low, provide additional relief for low-income families, or meet other pressing policy priorities. Restraining hidden spending through the tax code should be a goal that unites those who want existing government programs to be more effective and those who favor a smaller and less intrusive government.

NOTES

1. A fully comprehensive income tax base would include all net income of individuals, defined as the sum of an individual's consumption plus change in net worth, or saving. This tax base would include all real gains from assets in the year they are accrued, would impute all corporate income to individual shareholders (with no separate corporate income tax), would exclude inflationary gains and losses, and would count as income the imputed rental value of owner-occupied homes and consumer durables. The OMB/JCT baselines depart from this concept in some major ways. They allow for exemptions of components of income that are considered impractical to tax, such as accrued but unrealized capital gains, leave room for a separate corporate income tax, and permit the taxation of purely inflationary gains as well as deduction of the inflationary component of interest payments.

2. We recognize that President Bush also proposed major reductions in income tax rates, marriage penalty relief, and elimination of federal estate and gift taxes. We also recognize that rate reduction, marriage penalty relief, and cuts in estate tax accounted for most of the revenue losses from the tax bill of 2001. Consideration of these proposals is beyond the scope of this report, which focuses on special exceptions to the income tax, not general tax rules. If there are to be reductions in income taxes, however, rate reductions are superior to most targeted benefits.

3. For an analysis of the distributional effects of tax expenditures, see the paper by Michael Ettlinger in this volume.

4. The Joint Committee on Taxation (JCT) recently issued a report on ways to simplify the tax system. See Joint Committee on Taxation, *Study of the Overall State of the Federal Tax System and Recommendations for Simplification Pursuant to Section 8022(3)(B) of the Internal Revenue Code of 1986* (Washington, D.C.: U.S. Government Printing Office, 2001). JCT lists "the use of the Federal tax system to advance social and economic policies" as one of the major sources of complexity in the tax law.

5. Technically, it is sometimes preferable to use deductions instead of credits for some business incentives, particularly if the goal is to reduce the

effective tax rate on investment or to move partially toward a consumption tax. It has been shown, for example, that partial expensing of investments is more neutral in its treatment of assets with different economic lives than an investment credit.

6. These selections are endorsed by most of the Working Group, but some members disagree with some of the items in these lists, see merit in some of the tax breaks on the two lists, or have other favorites.

7. OMB Circular A-11 contains the following directive to executive branch agencies: "You must consult with the Office of Tax Analysis, Department of the Treasury, on all proposals for new or modified taxes or tax expenditures. After consulting with the Office of Tax Analysis, submit a justification of the proposal to OMB. The justification should include the views of the Office of Tax Analysis and address the following items: the nature and extent of the problem addressed by the proposal, the reason a subsidy is needed, the non-tax alternatives, and the reason a tax change is preferable to the non-tax alternatives. In addition, you should be prepared to submit justifications for continuing or reenacting existing taxes and tax expenditures in the program areas for which you have primary responsibility. Such justifications will contain the information described above." See Jacob J. Lew, director, "Preparing and Submitting Budget Estimates," Circular A-11, revised transmittal memorandum no. 73, Office of Management and Budget, July 19, 2000.

Evaluating Tax Incentives as a Tool for Social and Economic Policy

Eric Toder

1

Introduction

Traditional approaches to tax policy consider what are the fairest and least costly ways to apportion the cost of paying for public services among the population. By this standard, a good tax system should impose equal burdens on taxpayers in equal economic circumstances and larger burdens on those with more ability to pay tax. It should interfere as little as possible with household and business decisions concerning how to earn a living, what goods and services to consume, and where to invest, except when there are clear and identifiable market failures. It should be designed so as to minimize costs to taxpayers of complying with the law and costs to the tax collection agency of administering it. All major tax reform proposals over the past quarter century have endorsed these general principles.[1]

Acceptance of these broad principles, of course, does not produce a consensus on critical features of how a tax system should be designed. Advocates of major structural reforms differ in how they define fairness, in their assessment of the effects of taxation on economic behavior, and in the relative weights they assign to the goals of equity, efficiency, and simplicity. These differences lead to major variations among tax proposals, such as whether the tax base should be income or consumption and how graduated the rate structure should be.[2] But all the major tax reform advocates claim their proposals would advance the three above-mentioned goals.

The views in this paper represent those of the author and do not necessarily reflect the views of the U.S. Internal Revenue Service, the Urban Institute, its board, or its sponsors, or any other institution with which the author has been affiliated.

In contrast to the general guiding principles of tax policy, the U.S. income tax has since its inception, and especially since becoming a mass-based tax during World War II, been used to promote social and economic objectives as well. There are long-standing provisions in the income tax that encourage homeownership, subsidize the provision of group health insurance by employers, encourage retirement saving, and subsidize activities by state and local governments and charitable organizations. The income tax has provided favorable treatment of capital gains throughout almost its entire history and has always included provisions, varying over time, that encourage investments in selected industries and categories of assets.

The use of tax incentives to promote social and economic objectives has become more frequent in recent years. Most noteworthy has been the expansion in the use of the tax system to promote social policy objectives—education, health, retirement saving, housing, investment in economically disadvantaged areas, and support for low-income families and families with children. For example, in 1990 and 1993, Congress enacted major extensions of the earned income tax credit. The earned income credit now provides as much assistance as programs such as food stamps and Supplemental Security Income (SSI) and more than Temporary Assistance to Needy Families. The Taxpayer Relief Act of 1997 introduced new tax credits for expenses of postsecondary education and a new, partially refundable child credit.[3] It also broadened incentives for saving for higher education, expanded eligibility for tax-advantaged individual retirement accounts (IRAs), and expanded incentives for businesses to invest in economically depressed areas and to employ disadvantaged workers. Subsequent proposals by presidents from both parties have continued the trend toward using the tax system to promote social and economic policy objectives. For example, President Clinton's fiscal year 2001 budget included numerous new and expanded tax incentives. Among these were proposals to expand the earned income credit and the credit for postsecondary educational expenses, to increase the dependent care credit and make it refundable, and to introduce new, refundable credits for contributions to retirement saving accounts and expenses for long-term care. President George W. Bush's first budget also proposed to expand tax incentives. Among the many new and expanded tax incentives in the first Bush budget were proposals to make charitable contributions deductible for taxpayers who do not itemize deductions, expand educational savings accounts, introduce a new tax credit for health and insurance, and make the already existing research and experimentation credit permanent. (In the recent tax bill, enacted just before completion of this paper, Congress included only some of the president's proposals for new tax incentives but added others that were not in the president's budget.)

These and other special tax provisions are often referred to as "tax expenditures" in recognition of the fact that they substitute for direct spending programs as ways of advancing federal policy goals.[4] The Office of Management and Budget (OMB) defines tax expenditures as "revenue losses due to preferential provisions of the Federal tax laws, such as special exclusions, exemptions, deductions, credits, deferrals, or tax rates." OMB refers to these provisions as "alternatives to other policy instruments, such as spending or regulatory programs as means of achieving Federal policy goals."[5] The Treasury Department published the first list of federal tax expenditures in 1968. In response to a mandate that originated in the Congressional Budget Act of 1975, which established the congressional budget process, both OMB and the Joint Committee on Taxation (JCT) now publish annual lists of tax expenditures and estimates of their revenue losses. (The U.S. Treasury Department provides the estimates for the OMB publication.)

The growth in tax expenditures raises a number of serious issues for tax and budgetary policy:

- Does the use of the tax system for nontax objectives create a bias for too many government programs?

- Are programs more or less efficient and effective as tax subsidies instead of direct spending?

- Is the growth of tax expenditures making the tax system too complicated?

- Should there be any changes in the budget process to restrain tax expenditures?

This paper reviews the growth in the use of tax expenditures and assesses the pros and cons of using the tax system as a way of promoting social and economic policy objectives. Chapter 2 briefly reviews trends in tax expenditures and discusses how political incentives may lead to substitution of tax provisions for direct spending. Chapter 3 discusses issues in identifying and measuring tax expenditures. These questions, although apparently arcane, matter because any process to control or limit tax expenditures relies on reaching a consensus on how to define and measure them. Chapter 4 discusses considerations in evaluating the effectiveness of subsidies and transfers, whether in the form of tax benefits or direct spending. Chapter 5 discusses criteria for determining whether a particular program should be structured as an outlay or a tax incentive. Chapter 6 considers whether it makes sense to enact limits on tax expenditures.

2

THE RISE IN SPENDING
THROUGH THE TAX CODE

THE GROWTH AND REDIRECTION OF TAX EXPENDITURES

There are numerous conceptual difficulties in measuring tax expenditures and further problems in summing up individual tax expenditure items to compute a measure of total federal "spending" through the tax code. Thus, one cannot provide precise measures of the growth in tax expenditures relative to gross domestic product (GDP) or other budget aggregates. Available evidence suggests, however, that tax expenditures have been growing faster than the economy in most years since 1967, the first year in which government agencies began compiling tax expenditure data.

OVERALL GROWTH OF TAX EXPENDITURES

Some analysts have measured the growth of tax expenditures by summing official estimates for individual provisions reported by the Office of Management and Budget (OMB), the Joint Committee on Taxation (JCT), and the Congressional Budget Office (CBO). As discussed in the following section, such calculations may overstate or understate total tax expenditures because they do not take account of interactions among separate provisions.

Based on a Congressional Budget Office study, Stanley Surrey and Paul McDaniel reported that tax expenditures increased much faster than both GDP and direct outlays between 1967 and 1982.[1] Using OMB data, the author himself estimated that tax expenditures rose only slightly faster than GDP between 1980 and 1999.[2] Tax expenditures climbed sharply following enactment of the 1981 tax cuts, which included greatly expanded incentives for business investment. Then the Tax Reform Act of 1986 reduced special tax expenditures by lowering marginal tax rates and broadening the tax base. Several major tax breaks were eliminated, including the exclusion from income of capital gains and the investment tax credit; the lower rates reduced the cost of deductions and exclusions that remained in the tax law. Since 1990, tax expenditures have renewed their growth as new preferences have been added to the income tax, old ones have been widened, and tax rates have increased.

Shift of Emphasis from "Business" to "Social" Tax Incentives

The composition of tax expenditures also has changed over the past twenty years.[3] Tax expenditures can be classified as one of two types—"business" and "social" tax expenditures. "Business" tax expenditures are those that intend to promote investment generally or to help certain industries that Congress considers important for economic growth or national security. These include items such as the partial exclusion of capital gains from income, accelerated depreciation for investments in machinery and equipment, and tax incentives for energy production and conservation. "Social" tax expenditures are those that promote education, health, housing, retirement security, and income security for low-income families. Examples are the exemption of employer contributions for health insurance, the low-income housing tax credit, and credits for the expenses of postsecondary education. Using this definition, social tax expenditures have increased as a percentage of GDP since 1980, while business tax expenditures have declined. The growth of social tax incentives has been especially pronounced since 1990, while business tax incentives, which were cut sharply by the Tax Reform Act of 1986, have continued to decline as a percentage of GDP.

There are still several large business tax expenditures, however. According to OMB estimates, four business/investment tax expenditures each cost more than $10 billion annually in fiscal years 2001–2005. These provisions are capital gains ($43 billion in 2002), accelerated depreciation of machinery and equipment ($33 billion in

2002), step-up in basis for capital gains at death[4] ($29 billion in 2002), and exclusion of interest on life insurance saving ($17 billion in 2002). Many other provisions, although small in magnitude, are nevertheless important because they provide a large subsidy in relation to the dollar amount of activity receiving assistance.

POLITICAL INCENTIVES FOR USE OF THE TAX SYSTEM

Tax incentives are popular because they represent a way of increasing federal support for popular social and economic goals while giving the appearance of tax cuts instead of increases in spending. Compared with direct outlay programs with similar goals, they better meet the need of politicians to appear to favor spending restraint. Budget rules also may make it easier to enact tax incentives than comparable outlay programs. But, it is inaccurate to say that there are no fiscal restraints on tax incentives. Moreover, the incentives that congressional budget rules provided through most of the 1990s for using the tax system to promote the goals of spending programs may not work the same way in today's changing fiscal environment.

A LABELING PROBLEM

The share of federal spending as a percentage of GDP is the most visible measure of the size of government fiscal intervention in the economy. Keeping spending growth down provides the appearance that government is becoming smaller and less intrusive. In its fiscal year 2001 budget, for example, the Clinton administration took credit for reducing spending from 22.2 percent of GDP in 1992 to 18.7 percent of GDP in 1999.[5] Using tax incentives instead of spending to promote social policy initiatives helps keep this readily measurable share of government spending low.

BUDGET RULES

In recent years, budgetary rules may have contributed to the growth of tax expenditures as well. Since the enactment of the Omnibus Budget and Reconciliation Act of 1990, discretionary spending programs have been subject to an overall ceiling. The cap on discretionary spending drives program advocates to propose tax incentives to accomplish their goals because tax incentives do not require offsetting reductions in other discretionary programs to avoid breaching the cap. For most of the 1990s, Congress largely complied with the spending ceilings it had enacted in 1990 and extended in 1993. But after budget surpluses emerged in the late 1990s, both Congress and the executive branch were unwilling to conform to the much tighter ceilings put in place in the 1997 Balanced Budget Act.[6] With less restraint on discretionary spending, there is less incentive to use tax incentives as a substitute.

Tax incentives, however, must still compete with other fiscal measures for scarce federal dollars even though there is no specific limit on tax expenditures. Under the pay-as-you-go (PAYGO) limits in the budget process, any tax cut or increase in mandatory spending must be matched by an offsetting budgetary saving in other tax provisions or mandatory spending. This means that the budget rules force tax incentives to compete directly with other tax and entitlement provisions instead of discretionary spending.

Whether and in what form the PAYGO rules survive in today's changing fiscal environment remains to be seen. On the one hand, if the PAYGO rules are relaxed and less stringent but more realistic discretionary caps are instituted, political incentives for using the tax system for programmatic purposes could increase. On the other hand, if the discretionary caps are eliminated or routinely ignored, then there will be no budgetary pressure spurring the use of tax incentives in place of spending.

3

MEASURING TAX EXPENDITURES
WHEN IS A TAX BREAK A DISGUISED
SPENDING PROGRAM?

While the Office of Management and Budget (OMB) and the Joint Committee on Taxation (JCT) publish lists of tax expenditures annually, tax expenditures for individual items are not combined to display their overall revenue cost (taking into account interactions among provisions that reduce the total) or integrated in any other way into budget presentations. In part, this reflects the existence of considerable controversy over what should be counted as a tax expenditure and how its cost should be measured.

The fundamental problem is inherent in the definition of tax expenditures as "*special* exclusions, exemptions, deductions, credits, deferrals, or tax rates." To determine a tax expenditure, one needs to establish a baseline tax structure compared to which some provisions are exceptions. Inevitably, choosing which provisions are part of the baseline structure and which ones are exceptions involves many subjective judgments.

Treasury and JCT use similar definitions of the baseline tax, although there are some differences in detail. For both agencies, the baseline tax follows the concept of a "normal tax" originally developed by the Treasury Department in the 1960s under the leadership of Stanley Surrey.[1] This baseline is meant to represent a practical and broad-based income tax that reflects the general and widely applicable provisions of the current federal income tax. The normal tax is not a conceptually pure tax that includes all net income in the tax base once. It excludes some items of income—such as accrued but unrealized capital gains and imputed rental income from owner-occupied homes—on the grounds that including them in the tax base would be administratively unfeasible. It includes as part of the baseline provisions that overstate income, such as the taxation of gains that represent inflation and the double taxation of corporate dividends. Personal exemptions, standard deductions, and graduated individual tax rates are treated as part of the normal tax, on the grounds that a broad-based income tax can be progressive and can provide appropriate adjustments for family size. But graduated corporate tax rates are treated as a preferential item that favors small business.

THE TWO ROLES OF THE "TAX EXPENDITURE" LISTS

The numbers displayed on the tax expenditure lists serve two very different purposes. The first is the one implied by its name—to display the fiscal cost of provisions that could be designed as expenditures but that Congress has chosen instead to fund through exceptions from the tax law. Examples are the low-income housing credit and the alternative fuel production credit. Listing these provisions serves a budgetary control agenda because it prevents Congress from disguising the cost of spending programs that would otherwise be "hidden" in the tax code.[2] The second is to display the fiscal costs of all provisions that represent departures from proper income measurement, even if they do not have an obvious programmatic spending counterpart. An example is the exemption from tax of capital gains on assets transferred at death. Enumerating these items provides a "hit list" for tax reformers who want to advance goals of fairness and neutrality in the income tax.[3]

MEASURING THE COSTS OF "EXPENDITURE-LIKE" PROGRAMS

It is possible to design tax incentives that have virtually the same economic effects as just about any spending program. For example, David Bradford illustrates how one could slash both taxes and defense spending without sacrificing defense.[4] In the "Bradford Plan," the weapons appropriation would be cut to zero, but to offset this the Congress would enact a "weapons supply tax credit" (WSTC). To qualify for the WSTC, defense contractors would deliver the appropriate weapons to the Pentagon in exchange for certificates that they could redeem as credits against income tax.[5]

While the Bradford example is intended to be farcical, the proposal for school modernization bonds (SMBs) in President Clinton's last three budgets would have used a similar type of device to help local communities build schools. SMBs would expand a provision for Qualified Zone Academy Bonds (QZABs) that Congress enacted as part of the Taxpayer Relief Act of 1997.[6] In March 2001, Representatives Nancy Johnson (R-Conn.) and Charles Rangel (D-N.Y.) introduced a new bill to provide federal tax credits to pay the interest costs on $25 billion of SMBs.

A more straightforward proposal to aid school construction might request that Congress appropriate funding for interest subsidies and develop criteria for selecting school districts to receive the subsidized loans. The Department of Education would administer the program and make payments to cover the interest costs for the selected districts. The proposals for school construction bonds are equivalent to this hypothetical new spending program in all respects but one. In the tax proposals, instead of receiving interest payments from the Department of Education, qualifying school districts (selected by the same criteria as in the hypothetical spending example) would receive certificates to issue SMBs. The SMBs would pay no interest, but holders of the SMBs could claim tax credits in lieu of the interest receipts. The economic effects of this tax incentive are virtually the same as for the hypothetical spending program, but the budget proposal is scored as a tax cut instead of new spending.[7]

More generally, many provisions on the tax expenditure lists could easily be designed as direct spending programs.[8] But other provisions do not have an obvious spending counterpart. Some commentators believe that the tax expenditure list should be limited to provisions that meet two conditions:

- There is a general rule in the existing tax law, compared with which the specific tax provision is an exception.

- It is possible to formulate an expenditure program that would achieve the same objective as the tax provision.[9]

Under these criteria, the SMBs and QZABs would clearly be tax expenditures because they are not part of the general provision of the tax laws and they have a clear and obvious spending counterpart (an interest subsidy administered by the Department of Education). Many other items on the tax expenditure list clearly meet these criteria. But other provisions do not.

In the early 1980s, the Treasury Department developed the concept of a "reference" law baseline, which was meant to represent general rules in the current income tax instead of rules with a normative content. The intent was to distinguish departures from the normal tax that could be considered "tax expenditures" from those that fully or partially exclude some forms of income from the tax base, but do not clearly substitute for a spending program. For several years, the OMB/Treasury tax expenditure list excluded some major items that the JCT continued to list as tax expenditures. The changes were controversial, and, in response to objections, Treasury in 1984 began displaying all tax expenditures relative to the normal tax baseline, with a separate line for some items showing a value of zero relative to the reference tax baseline.[10]

MEASURING THE COSTS OF DEPARTURE FROM AN "IDEAL" TAX SYSTEM

Another purpose of the tax expenditure list is to indicate how much revenue is lost because the current U.S. tax system departs from a measure of a comprehensive but practical income tax base. The tax expenditure list helps inform an agenda for tax reform by displaying the costs of departures from this "normal" tax baseline.[11] For this reason, the tax expenditure list has often been used to enumerate items to be included in tax reform proposals. The Tax Reform Act of 1986, for example, eliminated numerous tax expenditures to pay for lower marginal tax rates for individuals and corporations.

Any departure from an ideal income tax will affect the allocation of resources and the distribution of after-tax income, regardless of whether it is measured against the normal or reference tax baseline. For this reason, the distinction between "tax expenditures" and "departures from ideal income measurement" is not conceptually clear. Stanley Surrey and Paul McDaniel reject the usefulness of distinguishing between these two types of provisions. They term the reference tax baseline as "highly idiosyncratic and inconsistent with tax theory, tax expenditure analysis, and the statutory definition adopted by Congress in the 1974 Budget Act."[12]

What Is the Proper Baseline?

Current State of the Debate

Currently, the normal tax base concept as originally designed by Surrey is the one used in the official tax expenditure lists, although footnotes in the OMB tables and discussion in the text still cite the alternative reference tax baseline. The tax expenditure list continues to serve as a menu for potential tax reforms but does not play an important role in influencing budgetary presentations.

Problems in Measuring Tax Expenditures

Notwithstanding the general acceptance of the normal tax concept, there remain many unresolved debates in the measurement of tax expenditures. These include general issues in defining the normal tax, the treatment of "exceptions to exceptions," the distinction between "revenue losses" and "outlay equivalents," and "timing" issues. Appendix 1 to this paper discusses these conceptual and measurement issues.

Evaluation

There is a clear need for accounting for the amount the government effectively "spends" in support of programs that are cleared through the tax system. There also is a constant need to reexamine provisions of the overall tax structure, which in many ways depart from criteria of efficiency, fairness, and simplicity. The published tax expenditure lists display the costs of many expenditure substitutes and provide much useful information on the costs of other exceptions to a baseline that commands wide, if not universal acceptance, as a model of a practical comprehensive income tax. But, because they serve dual goals—tax reform and spending control—they can supply misleading information for those seeking either one.

There are serious problems with including many items enumerated as tax expenditures on a "hit list" for tax reform. Eliminating or reducing tax expenditures to pay for lower rates is a common feature of tax reform proposals. But "spending" cleared through the tax accounts cannot be viewed simply as a defect in the tax system. For example, the exemption of employer-paid health insurance premiums from tax is a clear departure from proper income measurement rules in a broad-based income tax. But, in the absence of national health insurance, the exemption provides an important incentive for employers to provide group health insurance for their employees.[13] If the exemption were eliminated in the name of a pure tax system, there would be strong pressure to replace it with an alternative subsidy. More generally, reducing tax expenditures may do major harm to important social goals unless there is new direct spending or regulation. But, simply replacing tax expenditures with direct expenditures will not allow the large reduction in marginal tax rates that reform proposals promise.

There are problems likewise in characterizing some items that may belong on the tax reform agenda as disguised spending. Many items on the tax expenditure list do not have an obvious spending counterpart. But admittedly, the distinction between tax expenditures and nonexpenditure-like departures from a normal income tax is difficult to define with a set of objective criteria. One test may be the intent of the program—whether its purpose is to promote some well-defined activity that could be achieved through spending (like the proposed credit for SMBs) or to modify the general rules of an income tax (like the capital gains preference). But intent is often hard to discern, and many provisions serve multiple goals. Selecting which provisions are expenditure substitutes is a bit like deciding between pornography and art; you know it when you see it.

It would be useful, however, if alternative lists of tax expenditures were available that would classify them by different types. Some might be categorized as unambiguous spending substitutes, others as potential expenditure substitutes, and still others as provisions that represent nonexpenditure-like preferences in the income tax. It also would be useful to have estimates of aggregate revenue losses from subgroups of preferences, which would take account of interactions among provisions. This information would make for greater transparency in observing how policymakers are using the tax system to substitute for spending programs.

4

EVALUATING TAX EXPENDITURES

L abeling a program a tax expenditure does not in itself say whether it is a good or bad program. Like direct spending, tax expenditures alter the composition of goods and services produced in the economy and modify the distribution of after-tax income. These modifications may either improve or degrade economic efficiency and fairness.

It is useful to classify programs into two different general types—subsidies and transfers. Subsidies seek to change the pattern of economic activity, based on the idea that the value of some output is not fully captured by producers in private markets. (An example is basic scientific research, which is believed to generate knowledge and techniques with a social value greatly in excess of what can be captured by producers in private markets.) Transfer payments seek to raise the incomes of those with special needs. (Examples are family support payments for single mothers without other sources of income and Social Security benefits for retirees.) Some programs combine subsidy and transfer elements. (An example is tax credits or rent subsidies to make more housing available for low-income families.)[1]

As the discussion indicates, it is possible for programs with the exact same economic effects to be placed on either the tax or spending side of the budget. Frequently, the more interesting question is not whether a program is conveyed via tax breaks or direct spending but what design features it has.

Subsidies promote the production and consumption of selected goods and services by reducing their private cost of production through paying for part of the labor or capital used or by reimbursing purchasers for a portion of their spending. In the extreme, governments can pay for the entire cost of a good or service, making its consumption free to households.

Subsidies differ based on whether they:

- are based on the value of output of a good or the cost of inputs used in their production (labor and capital);

- are paid to business firms or households;

- are available to all or conditioned on the economic status of recipients;

- do or do not depend on whether the taxpayer has positive tax liability; and

- do or do not vary in magnitude with the marginal tax rate of the recipient.

Transfer payments raise the income and purchasing power of target populations. Some transfer payments simply provide cash, while others are intended to increase access of recipients to identifiable goods and services, such as food, housing, and medical care by reducing their cost. These latter programs have both transfer and subsidy characteristics.

Transfer payments differ based on whether they:

- provide benefits to all or only to those who meet needs tests, and, for the latter, how need is determined;

- are provided in the form of cash or in-kind benefits; and

- are or are not limited to recipients with positive earnings.

Appendix 2 of this paper elaborates on these design options for subsidies and transfer payments.

EVALUATING SUBSIDIES

There has been little discussion in the economics literature on criteria for evaluating tax subsidies (subsidies that take the form of tax breaks). The one test that usually has been used in the literature is whether the subsidies in fact induce more of the intended behavior. Thus, there have been a large number of papers that have examined the responses of taxpayers to particular incentives. Some of the articles directly estimate the effect of varying the tax incentive, and others use other evidence on price responsiveness to infer what the effects of tax subsidies might be. These papers have estimated, among others, the following responses:

- charitable contribution levels to the net-of-tax price of making contributions;

- capital gains realizations to the marginal tax rate on capital gains;

- homeownership rates to the mortgage interest deduction or alternative potential mortgage interest tax subsidies;

- business research and experimentation (R&E) spending to the R&E credit;

- employment of qualifying workers to the targeted jobs tax credit; and

- the level and composition of investment to the investment tax credit and other provisions affecting the cost of capital.

Martin Feldstein estimated that the elasticity of response of charitable giving to the price of giving (one minus the marginal tax rate) was greater than one.[2] That would mean the revenue loss from the deduction is less than the amount of additional giving it induces.[3] Feldstein interpreted this as evidence that the charitable deduction is more efficient than direct government support of the same activities. More generally, it is sometimes claimed that any tax expenditure is efficient if the dollar volume of induced activity exceeds the revenue loss.

But, evaluating a subsidy based on the size of the behavioral response it induces is surely incomplete and in many circumstances misleading. It avoids the basic question of whether the output generated by the tax subsidy is worth more to society than what it displaces. For example, suppose a tax subsidy is provided to industry X even though market prices accurately reflect the relative value to society of the output in X and in other industries. The subsidy, reduces the costs of X, causing its price to fall and leading more X to be produced and consumed. But with the presence of a subsidy, the social cost of producing X, in terms of the value of forgone output, exceeds its market value. In that case, a larger behavioral response corresponds to a larger efficiency loss from the subsidy, even if the induced gain in spending on X exceeds the federal budget cost.

Proper evaluation of a subsidy requires a careful statement of the subsidy's objectives and an assessment of the value of the additional outputs it generates, compared with the production it displaces. It also may require analysis of the incidence of a subsidy—that is, how the subsidy affects the after-tax distribution of income.[4] Finally, there should be an accounting for the value of resources used up in additional taxpayer compliance costs, costs of administration by the IRS and program agencies, and other transaction costs. Except for distributional analysis, such a broad assessment is rarely performed for tax incentives. (Static analyses of the effects of selected tax subsidies on the distribution of tax burdens among income groups *are* frequently produced by the Treasury Department, the Joint Tax Committee, and the Congressional Budget Office.) In contrast, government agencies have financed numerous studies of the effects of direct outlay programs within their sphere of responsibility. Many of these studies are careful evaluations that compare outcomes for target and control groups.[5] Since no agency "owns" the tax incentives in the sense that they must balance them against other programs in developing their budgets, there is no inducement inside the government to perform comparable evaluations of tax incentives. Some agencies, however, have examined tax incentives that affect activities within their area of responsibility.[6]

EVALUATING TRANSFER PROGRAMS

The primary purpose of transfer programs is to assist people with special needs. The most important criteria for evaluation are whether they are effective in raising the after-tax incomes of the target populations and whether they treat people with similar needs equally. But transfer programs may have unintended side effects, including adverse impacts on work incentives and family stability. Analysis of behavioral responses is therefore an important component of the evaluation process.

It is encouraging that the effects of the most important program to help the low-income population in the tax system—the earned income tax credit—are now being studied intensively by academic researchers and government agencies. Recently, there have been new studies on the consequences of the EITC for work effort by single mothers, for trends in marriage penalties, and for consumption patterns and saving by EITC recipients. In addition, there have been studies on sources of excess claims by EITC recipients.[7]

5

CHOOSING BETWEEN TAX SUBSIDIES AND DIRECT SPENDING

The effectiveness of any federal program depends much more on its specific design features than on whether benefits are paid in the form of a check from a program agency or a lower income tax liability. But administrative and functional conditions of a specific program may sometimes favor using the tax system as a vehicle for paying beneficiaries and sometimes favor the use of direct outlays.

HOW TAX AND DIRECT EXPENDITURES ALWAYS DIFFER

Involvement of the Internal Revenue Service. Tax incentives are claimed on tax returns. They alter the total amount of taxes paid or refund due at the end of the year and can affect withholding schedules and estimated payments. Individuals self-report their eligibility for tax benefits, subject to potential review and audit (with a low probability) by the IRS. Treasury and the IRS issue regulations that detail eligibility for the subsidy or transfer payment. In contrast, direct outlay programs do not require IRS involvement, other than the normal reporting of income generated from either government payments or purely private market activities.

Budgetary treatment. Direct outlay programs are displayed explicitly as government spending. The nonrefundable portion of tax incentives appears as an offset to taxes paid and is therefore indistinguishable from a reduction in tax rates in its effect on budgetary aggregates. The refundable portion of tax incentives that exceeds income tax liability, however, appears in outlay totals in the budget. (The only refundable provisions in current law are the earned income tax credit and part of the child credit.[1])

Accounting for costs of administration. The costs of administering direct expenditure programs appear explicitly as part of the budget of program agencies. In contrast, the cost of administering tax expenditures is not transparent. The additional complexity that tax expenditures add to the tax law raises the cost to the IRS of providing a given level of enforcement and taxpayer service. But the IRS budget does not break down costs into those attributable to tax expenditures and those attributed to provisions of the "normal" income tax. Moreover, one cannot determine the extent to which the incremental costs associated with tax expenditures cause the IRS budget to be bigger than it would otherwise be or instead reduce the quality of tax administration and taxpayer service from a fixed budget.

HOW TAX AND DIRECT EXPENDITURES OFTEN BUT NEED NOT DIFFER

Relationship of benefits to tax circumstances. Most tax incentives are not refundable and therefore cannot be used fully by all taxpayers. In addition, those tax incentives that are structured as exemptions or credits are worth more, per unit of subsidy base, to taxpayers in higher tax rate brackets. In contrast, the benefits of direct outlay programs typically do not depend on a taxpayer's bracket.[2]

Tax incentives can be made more like outlays by structuring them as credits and making them refundable. In some circumstances, tax incentives can be designed to assist individual and corporations with no tax liability without making them refundable. For example, a nonrefundable tax credit for wages can help low-income workers without tax liability if the credit is provided to the employer.[3]

Determination of eligibility. Eligibility for most tax incentives depends on characteristics of taxpayers or their economic behavior (such as investment in qualifying assets) that are specified in legislation. In contrast, eligibility for benefits under many outlay programs depends on choices made by program administrators, based on more general criteria. But some tax incentives also rely on program agencies either to certify eligibility or to select benefit recipients.

Degree of enforcement. Outlay program rules are usually enforced more stringently than those involving tax incentives. People have to file claims and sometimes appear in person before an administrator in order to receive a check. In contrast, people claim tax benefits on their returns; the IRS reviews eligibility only after the fact, either in the process of an audit or through checks of calculations on returns and their consistency with information supplied by third parties. (For some non-needs-based entitlements, such as Social Security, program benefits are computed administratively instead of being based on self-reporting.)

Self-reporting on tax returns deters fewer people, eligible or ineligible, from claiming benefits than outlay programs that require administrative approval before payment. In addition, for income-tested programs, the use of the tax system avoids the stigma associated with applying for public assistance. But the lower enforcement standard might result in more benefits being paid erroneously.[4] Congress could tighten enforcement of tax benefit claims by requiring some of the same checks that outlays require and by involving other agencies.[5] But, this would raise costs and might discourage some eligible recipients from claiming benefits.

Budgeted benefits or entitlements. Most tax incentives resemble entitlement programs in the sense that everyone who qualifies receives benefits. Total federal budgetary costs depend on program rules, economic conditions, and behavioral responses of individuals and businesses. In contrast, the cost of discretionary programs is set by congressional appropriations. But tax incentives can be, and sometimes are, structured as discretionary programs by subjecting them to program caps.

Required frequency of review. Most tax incentives do not require periodic congressional approval to remain in effect; in that way, they also resemble entitlement programs. In contrast, funding for discretionary programs is set annually, requiring Congress to make a decision every year to continue financing. Some tax incentives, however, have legislated expiration dates. Provisions subject to "sunset" include the research and experimentation (R&E) credit,[6] the work opportunity credit, employer-provided educational assistance, and the credit for orphan drugs.

Sunset provisions may facilitate better budgetary controls but do not necessarily do so. The expiring tax incentives mentioned in the previous paragraph have been extended on a regular basis, while some "permanent" incentives in the tax law have been eliminated or scaled back. Sunset provisions for tax expenditures may create a budgetary illusion by reducing their apparent long-term costs when in fact the provisions are so popular that they will never be permitted to lapse.

CRITERIA FOR CHOOSING BETWEEN TAX AND DIRECT EXPENDITURES

Some criteria are suggested here for deciding whether a program with a given economic design should be provided as a direct outlay or tax credit. In most circumstances, the choice should be dictated purely by administrative considerations. Tax incentives have special weaknesses, however, as a method of helping the lowest-income families, especially if there are constraints that prevent them from being made refundable.

MAXIMIZING ACCESS VERSUS MINIMIZING FRAUD

As noted above, the process of claiming a credit, deduction, or exemption on a tax return is usually easier and less costly for beneficiaries than the process of applying for and receiving assistance from spending programs. When individuals or businesses are already filing tax returns, a new incentive, even though it makes the tax law more complex, does not require a new point of contact between the citizen and a government agency.

Therefore, tax incentives are preferable when the most important priority is to maximize the number of eligible individuals and businesses that benefit. In contrast, if there is a relatively greater concern with potential for abuse, then an outlay program or a tax incentive with controls usually characteristic of outlay programs (such as precertification) would be the preferred approach.

DESIRED DEGREE OF ADMINISTRATIVE DISCRETION IN SETTING PRIORITIES

Many programs require detailed administrative review and judgments of experts in order to determine how best to spend public funds. For example, government grants for scientific research generally require reviews by panels of experts to determine what proposals are most promising and which funding options will produce the highest return. Such a program could still be made a tax incentive, with the review panel choosing projects and awarding grants in the form of a tax credit certificate. Such an approach would add an unnecessary level of administrative complexity. If the grant recipient already must supply detailed information to a program agency, the additional burden to that agency of writing a check would appear to be minimal.

In contrast, tax incentives may be preferable if the goal is to encourage more of a clear and broadly defined activity. Either a tax incentive or direct subsidy can lower the net cost of the activity, and, beyond that, market responses will determine how much additional activity occurs and by whom. If clear and objective eligibility criteria can be established (such as a subsidy that depends on the dollar value of home mortgage interest payments), then there is little point in channeling payments through a separate agency when the subsidy recipient already is settling an annual balance with the IRS. If, however, judgments need to be made by program experts on whether an expenditure meets the test for a subsidy (such as, for example, a subsidy for unspecified "energy-saving" equipment), then it might be better to have the subsidy administered by a program agency.

USE OF TAX RETURN DATA FOR ELIGIBILITY CRITERIA

Tax incentives are a preferable means of subsidy if eligibility criteria are linked to data already reported on tax returns. For example, if the intent is to condition a subsidy on an individual's income by, for example, denying it to high-income families, then it is easier to have the subsidy claimed on tax returns. (Subsidies that phase out with income may have adverse economic effects by raising marginal tax rates in the phaseout range, but these effects would be equally adverse for spending as for tax subsidies with the same phaseout rules.)

TARGETING BENEFITS TO LOW-INCOME INDIVIDUALS

Tax incentives have some major disadvantages as methods of helping low-income families. The main problem is political: the reluctance to make credits refundable and thus make more transparent the fact that they are really better viewed as spending than tax cuts. Another limitation is that the tax system works on an annual accounting period.[7] This makes it difficult to get benefits to recipients on a timely basis.[8] In contrast, many outlay programs provide benefits monthly.

CONCLUDING COMMENTS

Many programs can be designed as either tax breaks or outlays. Unlike direct outlays, tax benefits always affect annual net payments to the IRS and appear in budget presentations as tax cuts instead of spending. Tax incentives appear more attractive because they seem to reduce the size of government and because the costs of administering them are not transparent. Beyond that, the relative merit of using the tax system or direct outlays as a payment mechanism for any specific program depends on the relative costs of administration and compliance. In general, direct outlays are preferable to tax expenditures when there is a need to apply complex criteria to determine eligibility and, except for refundable credits, when the goal is to help low-income families and individuals. Tax expenditures are preferable to direct expenditures when one can establish objective and simple tests for subsidy eligibility and when income data currently reported to the IRS are useful for determining the amount of assistance.

6

POLITICAL INCENTIVES
SHOULD TAX INCENTIVES BE RESTRAINED?

The discussion in this paper suggests that there are political and budgetary incentives for excessive use of tax expenditures. Fewer budgetary constraints and lower standards of review than for spending programs makes it easy to create and expand tax expenditures even in cases where such measures are poor uses of taxpayer dollars. In addition, there is a tendency to use the tax system as a funding mechanism even when direct outlays are more efficient.

One possible response to these concerns is to enact an overall limit on tax expenditures. But there are other options short of strict spending caps.

DO OVERALL LIMITS ON TAX EXPENDITURES WORK?

Congress could set a total ceiling on tax expenditures, analogous to the ceiling on discretionary outlays. This ceiling could be established at the current level of tax expenditures or at some lower amount and could be allowed to increase with GDP, the price level, or some other economic indicator.

Overall limits on tax expenditures, however, are of questionable merit for several reasons. First, because many tax expenditures take the form of entitlements, it is not possible to forecast precisely their cost. Overall targets would have to be based on projections, and then programs would need to be adjusted after the fact if their costs exceeded estimates.

Second, as the discussion in Chapter 3 documented, there is considerable controversy about how to define and measure tax expenditures because there is no universally agreed-upon baseline tax system. Requiring the outcome of legislation to depend on the definition of tax expenditures confers enormous power on unelected civil servants. In addition, the current definition of tax expenditures renders them unacceptable for use as a device for preventing end runs around federal spending limits. This is because many tax expenditures represent departures from one definition of an ideal, though pragmatic, tax system rather than provisions that substitute for spending programs.

Nonetheless, Congress has in the past set ceilings on individual tax expenditures and could decide to cap selected groups of tax expenditures. In doing this, it could request that staffs prepare a list of those tax expenditures in particular program areas (housing, energy, health) that may potentially substitute for spending programs. While the decision on which items to include in the limits would inevitably be political, executive and legislative branch tax staff can and should pay an important role in developing proposed lists.

OTHER OPTIONS

Other options for preventing excessive use of tax expenditures include alternative reporting and measurement, requirements for periodic review of effectiveness, sunset, and limitations on entitlements.

Alternative reporting and measurement. As noted in Chapter 3, the tax expenditure lists published by OMB and JCT include both expenditure-like programs and departures from an ideal income tax base, although OMB does identify some items that would not be tax expenditures under an alternative concept. Agencies could be required to group tax expenditures into three categories: those that are clearly program substitutes, those that could be considered program substitutes, and those that are not program substitutes. (All the items should continue to be displayed on the list.) This additional information would facilitate public understanding of how much the tax law is being used to promote disguised spending. It also would be useful if the staff could calculate the revenue costs of groups of tax expenditures, taking account of interactions among them. This would reveal the aggregate spending through the tax system on different budgetary categories.

Requirements for periodic review and effectiveness. Although there have been a number of academic studies on aspects of selected tax incentives, the process for reviewing their effectiveness falls far short of the process for reviewing alternative spending programs. Congress could consider requiring that all proposed new tax incentives be accompanied by statements indicating their purpose, evidence that their design will lead to accomplishment of the goals at an acceptable cost, and a clear rationale for why a tax incentive should be employed instead of a spending program. Similar requirements could be imposed periodically on existing tax incentives.

Sunset. More tax expenditures could be subject to sunset provisions. This would require that Congress take positive action to continue them and, under current budgetary rules, would require that they identify other tax increases or spending cuts to finance them. As noted above, however, sunset has some disadvantages. It makes temporary tax expenditures look less costly than permanent ones, which is highly misleading if the provisions are so popular that Congress and the executive branch would never allow them to expire.

Limitation of entitlements. Some individual tax expenditure items that currently operate as entitlements could be made similar to discretionary spending programs by limiting their total funding. This would require that some state or federal agency select which qualifying taxpayers are eligible for the tax benefit. Examples of such tax expenditures in current law are the low-income housing credit and various tax-exempt bonds for private purposes. In both these programs, designated state and local agencies ration access to a federal benefit.

7

CONCLUSIONS

The use of tax expenditures to promote social and economic policy goals has been rising in recent years. Support for using the tax system in this manner is bipartisan. The Clinton administration enthusiastically promoted tax expenditures to help low-income families with children, support higher education, assist urban revitalization, and advance a host of other purposes. The Bush administration, although emphasizing across-the-board income tax rate cuts and elimination of the federal estate and gift tax, also has proposed expanding many tax incentives and creating new ones. Moreover, many proposals for new tax incentives originate in Congress, and the trend for members of Congress to propose more of them is continuing.

Politics and budgetary concerns make it easier to favor tax than direct expenditures. The result may be enactment of some tax subsidies that would be more cost-effective as direct spending and others that are best not enacted in any form. But many tax incentives support worthwhile public purposes. Eliminating them in the name of tax reform would be harmful unless they are be replaced by an alternative spending or regulatory program that meets the same goals.

Payments from many programs can be structured as either outlays from program agencies (spending) or tax rebates from the IRS (tax cuts) without changing their net effects on income distribution, the allocation of resources, or the federal deficit. Depending on the nature of the program, it may be either more or less costly to operate it through the tax system instead of as a direct outlay. Achieving government purposes by changing the tax law makes the tax code more costly for the IRS to administer and increases taxpayer compliance costs. But, in some circumstances use of the tax system may add less to the total public and private costs of administering government programs than a new spending program designed to achieve the same ends.

One cannot conclude that all tax incentives are either good or bad. The merits of tax provisions, like spending programs, need to be assessed on a case-by-case basis. But, overall, there are reasons for concern about the excessive use of the tax system as a method of providing subsidies. Because public discussion often obscures the fact that many tax incentives are really spending in disguise, it is often easier to enact unnecessary or ineffective programs in the form of tax incentives than as direct spending.

Institutional reforms to reduce biases that favor excessive use of tax breaks deserve consideration. Tax expenditure lists can be reformatted to highlight the differences between hidden expenditure programs and broad-based departures from a comprehensive income tax. The costs of groups of tax expenditures can be estimated simultaneously, including interactions among them, to reveal aggregates for budget categories that can be compared with spending totals for the same categories. More information about new and existing tax expenditures could be required as part of the legislative process and the development of executive branch budget proposals. This might include evidence on their effectiveness in achieving their objectives and a rationale for using the tax system instead of direct spending.

In short, tax incentives should receive the same level of scrutiny normally provided for spending programs. Given such scrutiny, many existing and proposed tax expenditures would be very difficult to justify.

APPENDIX 1

ISSUES IN MEASURING TAX EXPENDITURES

The Treasury Department and the Joint Committee on Taxation (JCT) define and measure tax expenditures as departures from a "normal" income tax. This paper has noted four problems in identifying and measuring the cost of tax expenditures: problems in (1) defining the "normal" tax, (2) classifying of "exceptions to exceptions," (3) distinguishing between "revenue losses" and "outlay equivalents," and (4) measuring tax expenditures that alter the timing of tax payments.

DEFINING THE "NORMAL" TAX

The normal tax is meant to represent a practical and broad-based income tax that reflects the general and widely applicable provisions of the current federal income tax. But, as noted in the text, the normal tax base departs from a truly comprehensive income base that includes all economic income of individuals (including income accrued within corporations). It excludes some items of income (imputed rent, accrued capital gains), includes some items that are not income (inflationary gains), and allows for a separate corporate tax on top of the taxation of individuals on their income from corporate dividends and capital gains on corporate stock. Some analysts believe that the normal tax should be a more philosophically consistent measure, such as comprehensive income. With comprehensive income as a base, tax expenditure estimates would provide a more accurate indication of how the income tax influences the allocation of resources, relative to a neutral system.

Other economists believe that a tax based on an individual's annual consumption is fairer and more neutral than a tax based on income.[1] Using a consumption tax as the normal base would alter several major items on the tax expenditure list. For example, under a consumption base provisions allowing exemption of income accrued within qualified pension plans—the biggest tax expenditure in the current list—would be part of the normal tax, not a tax expenditure.[2]

EXCEPTIONS TO EXCEPTIONS

Some provisions in the income tax limit deductions that are appropriate for measuring income, either as a simplification measure or as a way of restricting the use of explicit tax preferences. But some taxpayers are exempt from these limitations. It is unclear whether or not these "exceptions to exceptions" should be classified as tax expenditures. The argument for is that they provide special benefits for some taxpayers, relative to a more general rule. The argument against is that the provision does not itself cause the income of the taxpayer to be understated.

For example, the "passive loss" restrictions enacted in 1986 limited individuals from deducting losses on certain investments, even though business losses are normally deductible in a comprehensive income tax. The rationale for these limits was to prevent taxpayers from claiming losses on certain investments that often produced tax losses even when they were profitable because of other provisions that allowed the understatement of income. This raised the question of whether exceptions to the passive loss provisions (such as the exemption of oil and gas from the limits) should be considered tax expenditures. On the one hand, the exceptions did provide special treatment for certain industries. On the other hand, passive loss limitations would not be part of a full comprehensive income tax.

Another example was the treatment of investment expenses incurred by mutual funds and other regulated investment companies (RICs) after the Tax Reform Act of 1986. This legislation limited the itemized deduction for miscellaneous business expenses to amounts in excess of 2 percent of adjusted gross income. This was justified as a simplification measure, even though business expenses would be fully deductible under a comprehensive income tax. Under this provision, investment expenses incurred directly by taxpayers are subject to the 2 percent floor, but investment expenses incurred on the taxpayers' behalf by mutual funds and other RICs are in effect fully deductible. (Congress initially enacted a provision requiring taxpayers to report RIC expenses as income, with an offsetting miscellaneous deduction, but subsequently exempted RIC expenses from income.) Treasury and JCT counted the exemption of RIC expenses from income as a tax expenditure for several years, on the grounds that it was an exception to the general rule that business expenses are subject to a floor of 2 percent of adjusted gross income. They subsequently dropped the item from the lists, on the grounds that RIC expenses would be fully deductible under a comprehensive income tax.

OUTLAY EQUIVALENTS

OMB publishes both revenue losses from tax expenditures and "outlay equivalent" amounts. In some cases, the outlay equivalents are larger. The outlay equivalent measure intends to capture how much the subsidy might cost if it were a direct expenditure with the same resource allocation effects as the tax exemption. The basic insight is that outlay payments in return for services by firms and individuals are usually taxable income to the recipient, so that the cost must be "grossed-up" to include the tax paid on the outlay.

An example is the treatment of interest on tax-exempt bonds issued by state and local governments. The revenue-estimating convention assumes total income in the economy is fixed. The revenue loss is equal to the amount of exempt interest multiplied by the average marginal tax rate of holders of tax-exempt bonds. For example, if the tax-exempt interest rate is 7 percent and bondholders are in the 30 percent bracket, the revenue loss is 2.1 cents per dollar of bonds outstanding (.07 times .3). In contrast, the outlay-equivalent measure asks what the amount of a direct taxable subsidy to the borrower would have to be to reduce the after-tax return to 7 percent. It is then assumed that the bondholder would require a pretax rate of return of 10 percent to get 7 percent after tax. Therefore, the interest subsidy to the municipality would have to be 30 percent of the 10 percent return, or 3.0 cents per dollar of bonds. This is the "outlay-equivalent" cost because it provides the same after-tax return to the lender and cut in borrowing costs to the borrower as the exemption of interest.

TIMING ISSUES

Some tax expenditures alter the timing of recognition of income. This can produce a large subsidy even when the sum of taxable income across time periods is unchanged. For example, provisions to allow depreciation of capital at a faster rate than economic depreciation reduce taxable income from an investment in the first few years but then increase it later when deductions have been used up. In this way the present value of taxable income can be lowered significantly. Because the tax expenditure for depreciation compares annual receipts between current law and an alternative, slower depreciation schedule, accelerated depreciation for any single investment causes positive tax expenditures in the early years of an asset's life and negative tax expenditures later. (With investment growing, the positive tax expenditures from new investments will exceed the negative expenditures on old assets. But owing to changing provisions and uneven growth of some activities, the tax expenditure lists show negative amounts for some "timing" tax expenditures in some years.)

Use of annual revenue streams to quantify tax expenditures can mismeasure the relative size of tax expenditures that change the time pattern of tax payments. For example, back-loaded IRAs appear to cost less than front-loaded, deductible IRAs with the same or lower present value because they exempt future income instead of allowing an immediate deduction. In recognition of this problem with cash flow figures, OMB also publishes a table that shows the present value per dollar of investment for tax expenditures that affect the timing of tax payments.

APPENDIX 2

DESIGN ISSUES FOR TAX
EXPENDITURES

This appendix reviews optional ways of designing tax expenditures. It considers separately subsidies intended to alter the allocation of output and transfer payments intended to change the distribution of after-tax income.

DESIGN ISSUES FOR SUBSIDIES

SUBSIDIZING INPUTS OR OUTPUTS

An output subsidy directly reduces the price of a good, while an input subsidy reduces the price of capital or labor used in production. The school modernization bond (SMB) proposal discussed in the text is an input subsidy because it reduces the cost of capital (school buildings) used in education. The lifetime learning credit is an output subsidy because it directly finances a portion of tuition costs. Output subsidies are generally more cost-effective than input subsidies because they do not interfere with choices of the least-cost method of production, but sometimes it is more convenient to subsidize inputs. (For example, it is easier to subsidize the capital costs of school construction than to subsidize the output of public schools because the latter is not sold directly to consumers.)

Paying Subsidies to Business Firms or Individuals

Subsidy checks can be written to businesses or individuals. The subsidy will raise the price received by sellers relative to the price paid by buyers. The share of the gain received by each should depend on their relative responsiveness to price instead of on who receives the check. The SMB proposal is an example of a subsidy paid to individuals, in the form of an interest tax credit, although the intent is to reduce net interest costs of school districts. The alternative spending program discussed in Chapter 3 would pay the interest subsidy to the school district (the "firm" in this example). While the economic effects of paying subsidies to business or individuals may be the same, administrative convenience may favor one approach over another.

Open-Ended or Capped Subsidies

Subsidies can be provided to everyone who meets legislated criteria or can be subject to a budgetary cap, with public officials empowered to allocate funds among qualified recipients. Most tax subsidies are open-ended in that all who qualify can claim them; examples are the mortgage interest deduction and the exemption of interest on public purpose state and local bonds. But some tax subsidies are capped; examples are the low-income housing credit and the SMB proposal discussed above. An advantage of capped subsidies is that government can easily control their costs. A disadvantage is that they may not provide any marginal incentive for more activity, especially if the capped amount of activity is less than what is already occurring in private markets.[1]

Available to All or Conditioned on Economic Status of Recipients

Subsidies can be available to all who undertake the desired activity or can be limited based on economic status. An example of the former is the exemption of interest on state and local public purpose bonds. An example of the latter is the lifetime learning credit, which is phased out for taxpayers with adjusted gross income between $80,000 and $100,000.

CONDITIONED ON TAXPAYING STATUS OF RECIPIENT

Almost all income tax subsidies are conditioned on the taxpaying status of recipients because they are nonrefundable, that is, limited to the amount of positive income tax liability. The exceptions are the earned income tax credit and a portion of the child credit. The non-refundable nature of tax credits does not limit their value to high-income individual taxpayers and profitable corporations, who have enough tax liability to use the credits, but it does restrict their use by low-income individuals and unprofitable corporations. In contrast, subsidies in direct spending programs do not depend on the tax-paying status of recipients. Restricting subsidy payments to the tax li-abilities of recipients is one way of controlling their costs and may in some circumstances help enforcement agencies prevent them from being claimed by ineligible recipients. But for most subsidies there is little reason to make the amount of income tax payments a criteria for receipt of the benefit.

CONDITIONED ON MARGINAL TAX RATE OF RECIPIENT

For some tax subsidies, the subsidy rate per unit of activity varies directly with the marginal tax rate of the subsidy recipient. This condition holds for tax subsidies that operate by reducing the taxable income of individuals—whether through exclusions from income, deductions, or deferrals of income recognition. (Exclusions from corporate income also increase with the marginal rate of corporations, but this is less important because most cor-porate income is taxed at a flat rate of 35 percent.) Spending pro-grams never have this feature. Examples of such provisions are the mortgage interest deduction, the deduction for charitable contri-butions, and the exemption of interest on municipal bonds. Deductions make sense for expenses that can arguably be classi-fied as adjustments for ability to pay because then they serve the purpose of accurately measuring the appropriate tax base to which graduated rates should apply. But when correct income measure-ment is not an issue, it is almost never easy to justify providing larger marginal subsidy rates to higher-income taxpayers in a higher tax bracket. These provisions are sometimes termed "upside-down" subsidies because they assist those who need help the least. They can be converted into equal-percentage subsidies for taxpayers in all brackets by making them taxable credits instead of deductions.

DESIGN ISSUES FOR TRANSFERS

UNIVERSAL OR INCOME-CONDITIONED BENEFITS

Benefits intended to provide a social safety net may be universal or may be phased out or eliminated as incomes increase. For a given amount of assistance to low-income groups, universal benefits have a higher budgetary cost than income-conditioned benefits and therefore require higher marginal tax rates across the board to pay for them. But means- or income-tested benefits impose much higher marginal rates than universal benefits on those who are in the income ranges at which benefits phase out. Most tax expenditures with a transfer payment element are income-conditioned. (In contrast, major transfer programs on the outlay side, including Medicare and Social Security retirement benefits, are not conditional on a recipient's income.) Until the 1983 Social Security amendments, the exemption from income tax of Social Security benefits was available to all beneficiaries, but since then a portion of benefits has been taxable for taxpayers with income above a threshold amount.

MEASURING ECONOMIC STATUS

For benefits conditioned on need, there are alternative ways of measuring economic status. These include income or assets and can be defined for individuals, a family, or a taxpaying unit. Income can be measured annually or over shorter intervals. All tax expenditures with an income test use an annual income measure because the tax system does not collect information on either monthly income or wealth. But the specific measure varies among provisions. For instance, eligibility for the earned income credit is conditional on wages, adjusted gross income, and a separate test for investment income; the wage and income thresholds are the same for married couples and single individuals.

CASH OR IN-KIND ASSISTANCE

Assistance can be in the form of cash or cash-equivalent or in the form of specific goods and services, such as housing, food, or medical services. Tax expenditures are of both types: An example of the former is the child credit, which is strictly a cash grant. An example of the latter is the dependent care credit, which is an income-conditioned subsidy to help families purchase child care services.

WORK REQUIREMENTS

In recent years, there has been a trend toward requiring work as a condition for receipt of benefits. The earned income tax credit, which is income conditioned but goes only to taxpayers with some earnings, is an example of a social safety net program with a work requirement.

NOTES

CHAPTER 1

1. See, for example, the U.S. Department of the Treasury's 1984 proposals for broad-based tax reform, which were published as *Tax Reform for Fairness, Efficiency, and Simplicity* (Washington, D.C.: U.S. Government Printing Office, 1984).

2. There also are many other major design differences in reform proposals. Advocates of a consumption-based tax differ about the best method of collection (from retail sales, from all firms on a value-added basis, from firms and wage earners, or from individuals, with a deduction for saving) and about the treatment of international transactions (destination based vs. origin based). Advocates of income tax reform differ on how to adjust, if at all, for the double taxation of corporate dividends and the overstatement of capital income with inflation and differ on general rules for taxing foreign-source income of individuals and corporations.

3. A tax credit is called refundable if the amount a taxpayer may claim can exceed the taxpayer's positive income tax liability. Thus, a refundable credit can make net income tax liability a negative number.

4. The term "tax expenditures" and the concept of a tax expenditure budget were originally developed by Stanley Surrey, who was assistant secretary for tax policy at the U.S. Department of the Treasury in the 1960s. See Stanley S. Surrey, *Pathways to Tax Reform: The Concept of Tax Expenditures* (Cambridge, Mass.: Harvard University Press, 1973); Stanley S. Surrey and Paul R. McDaniel, *Tax Expenditures* (Cambridge, Mass.: Harvard University Press, 1985).

5. U.S. Office of Management and Budget, *Budget of the United States Government, Fiscal Year 2002: Analytical Perspectives* (Washington, D.C.: U.S. Government Printing Office, 2001).

CHAPTER 2

1. Surrey and McDaniel, *Tax Expenditures*.

2. Eric Toder, "The Changing Role of Tax Expenditures: 1980–99," *National Tax Association Proceedings: Proceedings of the 91st Annual Conference on Taxation* (1998).

3. Ibid.

4. People who inherit assets (stocks, real estate, etc.) can take as the asset's basis—that is, its deemed purchase price—the market value of the asset at the time they inherit it. This "step-up" in basis from its price when acquired by the decedent to its price when transferred at death eliminates any tax on capital gains accrued during the lifetime of the decedent.

5. *Budget of the United States Government, Fiscal Year 2001*, p. 26.

6. The caps have been circumvented through labeling some spending as "emergency" in nature and other devices. Some analysts believe that more realistic budget caps that allow spending to rise at the same rate as the price level or even at the growth rate of GDP would promote more fiscal discipline because it would be easier for Congress to comply with them. See the interview with Robert Reischauer in *Georgetown Public Policy Forum* 5, no. 1 (Fall 1999).

Chapter 3

1. This baseline tax is called the "normal" tax by the OMB and the JCT. OMB also uses an alternative baseline, the "reference" tax, which counts as exceptions only provisions that serve "programmatic purposes." In practice, this means that the tables in the budget include footnotes for those provisions that are tax expenditures only under the "normal tax" method.

2. Some commentators refer to these provisions as "hidden" in spite of their listing in the budget and in an annual JCT report because they receive much less attention than direct outlays in discussions of federal spending policy. Thus, a recent case study of the politics of selected tax expenditures by Christopher Howard is entitled *The Hidden Welfare State: Tax Expenditures and Social Policy in the United States* (Princeton, N.J.: Princeton University Press, 1997). Similarly, Citizens for Tax Justice calls its recent report on tax expenditures *The Hidden Entitlements* (Washington, D.C.: Citizens for Tax Justice, May 1996).

3. There has been a long-standing debate within the Treasury Department as to what end the tax expenditure list should serve. For an earlier discussion that highlights these two alternative purposes of the tax expenditure list, see Thomas Neubig, "The Current Role of the Tax Expenditure Budget in U.S. Policymaking" in Neil Bruce, ed., *Tax Expenditures and Government Policy* (Kingston, Ont.: John Deutsch Institute for the Study of Economic Policy, 1988).

4. David F. Bradford, "Tax Expenditures and the Problem of Accounting for Government," in Bruce, *Tax Expenditures and Government Policy*.

5. Of course, for the Bradford plan to be a perfect substitute for direct spending, the credit would have to be refundable. Alternatively, there could be some other device, like the safe-harbor leasing provisions in effect in

the early 1980s, to allow weapons-producing firms without sufficient income tax liability to use all the credits by "selling" them to other taxpayers. Bradford used his example to illustrate how the budget deficit could have been eliminated, without raising net taxes or sacrificing programs, by combining this spending/tax cut with an increase in other revenues.

6. For a discussion of QZABs, see Bruce Davie, "Tax Credit Bonds for Education: New Financial Instruments and New Proposals," *National Tax Association Proceedings*, 1998.

7. Again, the absence of refundability is the only difference between the tax proposal and its spending counterpart. Some taxpayers would be ineligible to claim the full benefit of tax credits from the SMBs because of insufficient tax liability and limitations on the use of credits. Presumably, SMBs would be purchased by taxpayers with enough tax liability to use the credits fully. If the program were a direct interest subsidy, the bonds would appeal to a different group of investors.

8. Of course, as the examples in the text suggest, it also is true that many existing spending programs could be designed as tax expenditures.

9. For a forceful exposition of this viewpoint, see Seymour Fiekowsky, "The Relation of Tax Expenditures to the Distribution of the Fiscal Burden," *Canadian Taxation* 2 (Winter 1980).

10. OMB currently displays (in footnotes) those proposals it would not call tax expenditures under the "reference law" baseline, which "limits tax expenditures to those that serve programmatic purposes." These include deferral of income from controlled foreign corporations, expensing of research and experimentation costs, special tax rates for capital gains, accelerated depreciation, expensing of certain small business investments, amortization of start-up costs, the graduated corporate tax rates, exclusion of scholarship and fellowship income, and exclusion of public assistance benefits.

11. The revenue gain for eliminating one or several tax expenditures is often not the same as the revenue loss from the expenditure for several reasons. One reason is that the estimates of the tax expenditure budget are made assuming current patterns of activity. But elimination of a tax expenditure provision could induce a behavioral response, which would shrink the revenue gain. A second reason is that tax changes are often phased in, so that the entire tax expenditure may not be eliminated for many years. For example, a proposal to eliminate preferences for a particular type of investment would usually only apply to new investments, leaving tax expenditures on old capital unchanged. A third reason is that tax expenditure estimates all assume that other provisions of the law are fixed. In fact, if one tax expenditure is eliminated, the costs of other tax expenditures could change. The Congressional Budget Office publishes an annual list of options for raising revenue, many of which would reduce tax expenditures, along with estimates of the revenue gains

from these options. See *Maintaining Budgetary Discipline: Spending and Revenue Options*, Congressional Budget Office, April 1999.

12. Surrey and McDaniel, *Tax Expenditures*.

13. For an analysis of the effects of removing this incentive on health insurance coverage in the context of tax restructuring, see Jonathan Gruber and James Poterba, "Fundamental Tax Reform and Employer-Provided Health Insurance," in Henry J. Aaron and William G. Gale, eds., *Economic Effects of Fundamental Tax Reform* (Washington, D.C.: Brookings Institution, 1996).

CHAPTER 4

1. This categorization is similar to the one used in the classic public finance text by Richard Musgrave. See Richard A. Musgrave, *The Theory of Public Finance: A Study in Public Economy* (New York: McGraw-Hill, 1959). Musgrave classifies fiscal policy effects into three types: on allocation of resources, distribution of income, and economic stabilization. The discussion in the text refers to the first two of these effects.

2. Martin S. Feldstein, "A Contribution to the Theory of Tax Expenditures: The Case of Charitable Giving," in Henry J. Aaron and Michael J. Boskin, eds., *The Economics of Taxation* (Washington, D.C.: Brookings Institution, 1980).

3. More recent work by Randolph has estimated much lower responsiveness than the earlier work of Feldstein and others. Randolph finds that much of the effect previously observed is a transitory response; taxpayers time their giving to coincide with tax years in which their marginal rate is lower. See William Randolph, "Dynamic Income, Progressive Taxes, and the Timing of Charitable Contributions," *Journal of Political Economy* 103, no. 4 (August 1995): 709–38.

4. One should not give too much weight to estimates of the distributional impact of individual tax subsidies whose main intent is to reallocate resources. What matters is the distributional burden of the entire tax system, taking into account both the tax base and tax rates—not the contribution of specific provisions to the overall distribution.

5. For a summary of social experiments in the areas of Aid to Families with Dependent Children, food stamps, Medicaid, health care, programs for preschool children, youth employment programs, programs to lower unemployment, wage subsidies, housing vouchers, substance abuse, mental health, assistance to the elderly, and aid to the homeless, see David Greenberg and Mark Shroder, *The Digest of Social Experiments,* 2d ed. (Washington, D.C.: Urban Institute Press, 1997). It is interesting to note that none of the evaluations reviewed in this volume relate to tax expenditures.

6. For example, over the years both the Treasury Department and the Department of Labor have performed a number of evaluations of the targeted jobs tax credit.

7. See Bruce D. Meyer and Dan T. Rosenbaum, "Making Single Mothers Work: Recent Tax and Welfare Policy and Its Effects," *National Tax Journal* 53, no. 4 (December 2000); Stacy Dickert-Conlin and Scott Houser, "Taxes and Transfers: A New Look at the Marriage Penalty," *National Tax Journal* 51, no. 2 (June 1998); Janet Holtzblatt and Robert Rebelein, "Measuring the Effect of the EITC on Marriage Penalties and Bonuses," *National Tax Journal* 53, no. 4. part 2 (December 2000); Timothy Smeeding, Katherin E. Ross, and Michael O'Connor, "The EITC: Expectation, Knowledge, Use, and Economic and Social Mobility," *National Tax Journal* 53, no. 4, part 2 (December 2000); Jeffrey Liebman, "Who Are the Ineligible EITC Recipients?" *National Tax Journal* 53, no. 4, part 2 (December 2000); Janet McCubbin, "EITC Noncompliance: The Determinants of the Misreporting of Children," *National Tax Journal* 53, no. 4, part 2 (December 2000).

CHAPTER 5

1. The 2001 Tax Act significantly expanded the circumstances under which taxpayers may claim refundable child credits.

2. In some cases, the value of outlays does depend on tax circumstances because the outlay is combined with a tax subsidy. For example, the tax exemption of military housing makes military housing allowances worth more (relative to other income) to recipients in higher tax brackets than to those in lower ones.

3. This assumes that the benefit of the credit is shifted to workers in the form of higher pretax wages. The work opportunity credit is an example of a tax subsidy designed to benefit nontaxpaying workers, even though it is not refundable.

4. John Karl Scholz and, in a separate paper, Stacy Dickert, Scott Houser, and Scholz estimate that a larger portion of eligible recipients receive the EITC than the proportion eligible who receive AFDC (as it then existed) and food stamps. But estimated excess claims also are higher for the EITC than for most welfare programs. See John Karl Scholz, "The Earned Income Tax Credit: Participation, Compliance, and Antipoverty Effectiveness," *National Tax Journal* 47, no. 1 (March 1994); Stacy Dickert, Scott Houser, and John Karl Scholz, "The Earned Income Credit and Transfer Programs: A Study of Labor Market and Program Participation," in James M. Poterba, ed., *Tax Policy and the Economy*, vol. 9 (Cambridge, Mass.: MIT Press, 1995).

5. For example, Congress has mandated that IRS expend more resources in enforcing the EITC.

6. President Bush has proposed to make the R&E credit permanent.

7. Taxpayers with positive liability can receive benefits before the end of the year by adjusting their withholding. In addition, the IRS will make advance payments (negative withholding) of the EITC available to employees

who sign up for the option with their employers. In the early 1990s the Clinton administration tried to promote the advance payment option so that recipients did not have to wait until they filed their tax returns to receive EITC payments. But the take-up rate on the advance payment option was very low, possibly because most low-income workers do not want to run the risk of having to make a large payment to the IRS the following April if they qualify for a smaller EITC than they anticipated.

8. Some analysts have argued that the lump-sum nature of the EITC is an advantage because, instead of using the cash to support monthly expenses, families use the money for saving, to purchase "big-ticket" items they could not otherwise afford, or to make investments (in schooling, transportation, or moving) that facilitate social mobility. See Smeeding, Ross, and O'Connor, "EITC: Expectation, Knowledge, Use, and Economic and Social Mobility"; Lisa Barrow and Leslie McGranahan, "The Effects of the Earned Income Credit on the Seasonality of Household Expenditures," *National Tax Journal* 53, no. 4, part 2 (December 2000); Jennifer L. Romich and Thomas Weisner, "How Families View and Use the EITC: Advance Payment versus Lump Sum Delivery," *National Tax Journal* 53, no. 4, part 2 (December 2000).

APPENDIX 1

1. See David F. Bradford and U.S. Treasury Tax Policy Staff, *Blueprints for Basic Tax Reform*, 2d rev. ed. (Arlington, Va.: Tax Analysts, 1984).

2. Still others have suggested that tax expenditures be measured relative to other federal taxes, such as excise or payroll taxes. For an illustration of what an "excise tax expenditure" base would look like, see Bruce Davie, "Tax Expenditures in the Federal Excise Tax System," *National Tax Journal* 47, no. 1 (March 1994).

APPENDIX 2

1. For example, a study by the Congressional Budget Office suggests that the low-income housing tax credit may largely benefit selected investors instead of increasing housing supply or reducing housing prices. See "Cost Effectiveness of the Low-Income Housing Tax Credit Compared with Housing Vouchers."

Tax Breaks and Behavior
A Review of Evidence

Bernard Wasow

Advocates of tax breaks typically invoke the salutary effects of tax incentives on the behavior of households and businesses. It is argued that tax breaks encourage thrift, hard work, and investment; that they protect jobs, encourage conservation, reward home ownership, and charity; that they increase production of good things like petroleum and timber. Sometimes, they are defended for their distributional effects, for their support of small business or the working poor. This paper will summarize the arguments often made to justify tax breaks and review and analyze evidence that tests the validity of these justifications. It will focus on the effects of tax breaks on saving, investment, and work. While it will have little to say about the effect on production of various worthy products, it will consider why there has been so little research on this topic.

RATIONALIZATIONS FOR TAX BREAKS

Superficially, the rationale for tax breaks is obvious: they encourage desirable behavior and productive activity. The issue becomes far more complicated when one asks why people do not engage in such behavior without tax incentives, or why they do not engage enough. These questions become more pointed when it is noted that good things usually come at a cost. Saving is good, but so is its alternative, consumption. Work is good, but so is leisure. Investment in homes is good, and so is investment in factories or highways. Petroleum is valuable, as is everything else that consumers pay for. People cannot spend their limited time or treasure on more of everything. To repeat

the central challenge, then, a government-provided incentive needs
to be justified by more than the claim that it encourages good behavior. Advocates must argue that too little of the good thing is de-
livered absent government incentives, or, more technically, that the
social benefits of encouraging a behavior outweigh the social costs.

The section of the 1998 federal budget that deals with energy
provides an example of the typical justification offered for tax breaks:

> [T]he Federal Government allocates about $3 billion a year
> in tax breaks mainly to encourage the development of both
> traditional and alternative sources of energy. . . . Federal tax
> incentives are mainly designed to encourage the domestic
> production or use of fossil and other fuels, and to promote
> the vitality of our energy industries and diversification of our
> domestic energy supplies. The largest incentive lets certain
> fuel producers cut their taxable income as their fuel re-
> sources are depleted. An income tax credit helps promote
> the development of certain non-conventional fuels.[1]

Superficially, this appears to be a plausible statement, but it is not
framed in terms that permit an economic evaluation. The statement
refers to the benefits of tax breaks for energy production and diver-
sification, but it says nothing about costs. Moreover, there is no attempt to argue that other economic incentives result in too little
"development of both traditional and alternative sources of energy."
Between every line of the statement is the unstated and undefended
claim that there are market failures in production of energy, failures
that require government subsidies.

One might expect the American system, with its strong commit-
ment to private enterprise, to proceed with the default assumption that
a market outcome is socially desirable. When measures to raise revenue
are introduced, these should be neutral, affecting incentives as uniformly as possible, unless there is an explicit case for deviation from
neutrality. But the arguments for tax breaks intended to encourage production of specific goods or investment in specific assets seem to be built
on a foundation that contradicts this idea. The assumption of market failure underlies almost every defense of tax breaks, yet it is never stated why
or how markets have failed. It is not possible to gauge the cost of the failure (and therefore the potential benefit of the remedy) nor the cost of
the remedy. In the case of energy, the $3 billion foregone in revenues

may succeed in encouraging development of traditional and nontraditional fuels, but it is never explained why such encouragement is necessary or what its effects are. There is no reason to be confident that the resources spent on fuels provide society with more benefits than if they instead were used to produce goods and services that do not enjoy public subsidies. It must be inferred that without special incentives the market somehow delivers the wrong mix of products.

Advocates of tax breaks imply four kinds of market failure. Markets produce

1. too little saving;

2. too little investment;

3. too little work effort; and

4. too little production of certain goods and services.

This paper will not go into detail on the fourth of these; it will make no effort to judge whether security or other considerations suggest that we would misuse our energy resources absent tax breaks. Nor will it consider whether tax breaks for mining, timber, insurance, or other interests can be justified rationally. It is not necessary to dissect each and every tax break; the unsophisticated defense typically offered for tax breaks for special interests—that worthy people or enterprises are helped—leads one to doubt that a convincing case could be made. Until economic analysis demonstrates market failure, it is reasonable to have suspicions about the legitimacy of tax breaks targeted at specific industries. Absent a convincing case to the contrary, the market should determine what is produced and how.

The discussion that follows will proceed as if the nation ought to have more saving, investment, and work. These assumptions may be treated as moot.

SAVING

Efforts to explain household saving usually begin from theory that assumes a rational household that uses saving to permit consumption to vary less, year to year over a lifetime, than income. In the standard model, a person is likely to consume more than he earns early in life and during retirement, saving in the middle years to make this possible. Almost every part of this theory of saving behavior has been questioned: Do people really look only at their own lifespans when they make saving decisions? Are they really as foresighted and calculating as the theory assumes? And, even if they would like to save as the model predicts, do the institutions of modern capitalism make this possible?

Goals. Many wealthy people behave as if they do not want to die with zero net worth. Whether they want to leave bequests or they derive other benefits from ownership, they do not spend down their wealth in old age. At the opposite end of the income distribution, many households save little or nothing during their working years. For all households, precautionary saving against the possibility of exceptional expenses also may play an important role in saving decisions. Deviations from a life cycle model, particularly among the richest families, might affect a far larger proportion of total saving than of total households.

Rationality. Consumption-smoothing and bequest motivations aside, economists' theories of saving assume a lot of sophisticated planning on the part of households. There is evidence that many people lack information, that they rely on rules of thumb, and that they do not always do what they say they would like to do.

Liquidity. For most households, the institutions they deal with make it easier to build up assets than to build up liabilities. Young people, in particular, may be constrained in how much they can borrow. Families facing a sudden crisis also might find it difficult to borrow against uncertain future income. A household in this situation might be unresponsive to incentives because it cannot do what it would like to do.

Regardless of the ultimate reason people save, most tax breaks to encourage saving aim to achieve this result by increasing the rate of return on saving. IRAs and the like all are intended to increase saving through favorable tax treatment of current income that is saved or income derived from saving (interest and dividends). It may be somewhat surprising, therefore, to recall that economic theory does not predict that an increase in the return to saving will increase the amount of saving. The theoretical effect of tax breaks on saving is ambiguous for a very simple reason. If income and wealth remained constant, then an increase in the return to saving would, in theory, unambiguously increase saving. But changes in the rate of return also affect wealth and this can feed back into saving decisions. For example, if someone has a target level of future wealth, then an increase in the rate of return might discourage saving rather than encourage it. There are historical examples of this: when real interest rates rose in the early 1980s, contributions to defined benefit pension plans fell, reducing rather than raising the saving rate.

Theory may provide a flimsy justification for tax incentives for saving, but changes in tax law are not driven by theory anyway. Is evidence more supportive of the "common sense" notion that households respond to a cut in the tax on capital income by saving more? In the aggregate, saving appears to be unresponsive to rate of return. Stanford University economist B. Douglas Bernheim summarizes the empirical literature as follows: "the estimates [of interest elasticity of saving] tend to cluster near zero."[2] Whatever motivates households to save, it does not seem to be sensitive to moderate changes in the rate of return on savings.

Turning to tax incentives specifically targeted to increase retirement saving, the evidence on aggregate effects is ambiguous, too. It is clear that households have taken advantage of the opportunity to create individual retirement accounts (IRAs) and 401k plans and that household portfolio choice is sensitive to tax rates.[3] But experts disagree concerning the effect of the growth of tax-sheltered accounts on total saving. While households with IRAs save more than households without IRAs, the direction of causality is uncertain; do tax breaks that reward saving simply identify those households that are inclined to save, or do the tax breaks lead to more saving? This dispute could be resolved by an experiment that offered tax incentives to only part of a group that is otherwise entirely homogenous, but no such experiment has been identified. Economists have come up with ingenious methods for finding natural experiments to answer similar questions, but none has been discovered for these data.[4] So the consequences of saving incentives for total saving continues to be a matter of dispute.

Similar ambiguity surrounds the effect of incentives on corporate saving. Tax policy toward dividends versus capital gains certainly affects corporations' decisions to retain earnings (save) or to pay dividends. The aggregate effect of this corporate decision depends on household decisions to save or spend out of various income streams, especially capital gains versus dividends. There is not enough evidence for differences in household saving from these income streams to justify a strong conclusion on the effects of corporate income retention policy on total private saving.

INVESTMENT

Economists' theories of the investment decision are far more elaborate and sophisticated than the standard theory of consumption. Unfortunately, they are only moderately helpful in predicting investment. Keynes invocation of investors' "animal spirits" seems as appropriate today as it was in the 1930s. Yet among the information that feeds investors' expectations, surely taxation plays a role. Thus, both of the major theoretical approaches favored by economists today predict that taxes should matter to the investment decision. Models in the neoclassical tradition focus on the cost of capital. Models that follow James Tobin's "Q" weigh the cost of capital goods against expectations of future profitability, as measured by stock prices. In both theories, taxes should matter, as they affect the cost of capital and share prices.

Policymakers appear also to have concluded that investment tax breaks spur investment: ". . . [M]any governments have apparently believed that tax policy can be used as an instrument to alter firms' capital investment decisions. Indeed, investment tax credits, special investment 'reserve' funds, or accelerated depreciation allowances have been the rule rather than the exception in most developed countries since World War II."[5] But is this belief justified? The authors continue: "Against this backdrop, however, economists have generally struggled to find a significant impact of tax policy on investment."

Models of investment behavior have performed somewhat better when complex adjustment cost considerations have been added to the theory and the estimated specifications. The consensus among economists, including Kevin A. Hassett and R. Glenn Hubbard (whose skeptical introduction is quoted above), is that taxes and tax breaks are important to investment decisions, but this conclusion is supported much more firmly by theory than by evidence. The strongest empirical regularity in investment data is the simple correlation between investment and the contemporary state of the business cycle. Compared to this regularity, there is modest support for the proposition that investment varies systematically with taxes.

One component of investment might be singled out for more careful consideration. Tax incentives for research and development (R&D) spending have been more variable than tax incentives for investment in equipment or structures, so the data are richer. The argument for market failure is also especially strong applied to R&D since much of the output of research, especially basic research, is a public good, the benefits of which are difficult for the researcher to appropriate. (Of course, the patent and copyright systems create intellectual property rights; one rarely encounters a careful case that these support insufficient R&D.) Early efforts to corroborate the predicted effect of R&D tax breaks on R&D spending produced results similar to those for investment more generally: it was hard to establish any effect. More recently, research that allows for long lags for R&D spending in response to tax breaks suggests that the effect is substantial. A survey in 1999 affirms optimistically: "In the current (imperfect) state of knowledge we conclude that a dollar in tax credit for R&D stimulates a dollar in additional R&D."[6] This optimism may reflect eagerness by researchers to establish what they have predicted. Every analytical consideration supports the notion that investors should increase their activity in response to tax incentives. Absent an alternative theory, research has found that tax incentives do increase investment, but the road to that conclusion has been rocky.

EFFECTS ON INVESTMENT OF CAPITAL GAINS AND ESTATE TAXATION

Taxation of capital gains and estates have long been an important focus of those who would like to expand tax breaks; many want to abolish these taxes entirely. Representative Jennifer Dunn (R-Wash.) expressed widely held views when she argued in Congress for such changes in the tax code. She and Representative Robert T. Matsui (D-Calif.) introduced "a bold proposal to zero out capital gains taxes for those who invest in our burgeoning high tech industry." On inheritance taxes, she is equally forceful: "no other provision, Mr.

Speaker, is as historic . . . as the elimination of the death tax. . . . Mr. Speaker, I urge my colleagues to support the Financial Freedom Act. It encourages savings, investment risk, and the creation of wealth. It is also time, Mr. Speaker, I believe, to honor our most fundamental values, not tax them."[7]

There is little economic research that measures the effect of these taxes on household saving or real investment. The capital gains tax certainly discourages churning of portfolios, but it is a long way from frequent sale and purchase of financial assets to real investment in machinery and buildings. Theoretically, there is no reason to expect that capital gains taxation should affect real investment except as it affects the cost of capital by encouraging saving, thereby changing the rate of interest. This is a tenuous connection. The effect of capital gains taxation on the rate of return on saving is ambiguous in theory and hard to discover in data. A recent review of the evidence concludes as follows:

> a cut in the tax rate on capital gains is unlikely to have much effect on saving and investment because saving is relatively unresponsive to tax incentives, capital gains are a small part of the overall return from saving, and businesses require lower costs of capital in order to use the additional savings that are generated. Moreover, . . . there is still a relatively large revenue cost for cutting tax rates on capital gains.[8]

In spite of weak evidence, tax breaks on capital gains are popular not only among people who enjoy high capital gains, the wealthy, but among those whose income depends on turnover in asset markets, financial brokers.

The effects of estate taxation on saving and work effort are likewise ambiguous in theory and obscure in data. Estate taxation is especially complicated because it affects two generations: an older generation, who makes bequests, and a younger generation, who receives them. In general, whatever effect estate taxation may have on saving and work effort can be expected to be opposite in the two generations: if an increase in the estate tax discourages saving and work among old people, the same reasoning suggests that it should increase saving and work among those who now inherit less. In fact, the effect on neither the old nor the young is large and clear enough to provide strong empirical results.

Along with the political pressure to eliminate capital gains and inheritance taxes, there is considerable support for removing the remaining taxation of capital income. A number of variations of the flat tax or consumption tax pursue this goal systematically. While such comprehensive tax reform is beyond the scope of this review, it, like the reduction of the capital gains tax rate and the elimination of estate taxes, is justified by projected effects on saving that are difficult to corroborate with data. So while Representative Dunn's position that "death taxes . . . dishonor our most fundamental values" cannot be countered with evidence on saving and investment, the argument that tax breaks on capital income result in more saving, investment, and wealth creation is not well supported by evidence.

WORK

For work effort, as for saving, the theoretical connection to taxation is ambiguous. A reduction in the rate of income taxation increases the reward to work, but it also increases income at every level of work effort. Since leisure is something almost everyone values, workers can be expected to take part of the increase in earning power in more leisure, less work. Certainly the history of the workweek suggests that a higher rate of return to work does not necessarily increase the amount of work. As the real take-home wage grew steadily over the twentieth century, workers opted for a shorter, not a longer, workweek. The same is true of working years; age at retirement has been falling as wage rates have increased.

Over the past few years, we have been engaged in a major social experiment regarding work incentives, an experiment that may shed light on how tax incentives, along with other incentives, affect hours of work. With welfare reform, policy has shifted from support of nonworking mothers to support of the working poor. One of the most important consequences of this shift is for employment of low-skilled workers. The importance lies not in the boost to output—which is likely to be small because the number of workers is relatively low, as is their productivity—but rather the effect of our shift in income support policies on social attitudes and norms. Many more Americans sympathize with the working poor than with the nonworking poor. Thus the earned income tax credit (EITC) has grown to become our largest need-based income transfer program rather quietly, with relatively little partisanship. How much has this shift increased work among the poor? More generally, what do we know about the response of work hours to changes in the tax/transfer system?

Theory leads to only two certain predictions about the effects of taxes and subsidies on hours of work. First, income received independently of hours worked should reduce hours worked. (This follows from the assumption that people value leisure along with other goods and services.) Second, a marginal tax rate of 100 percent or more should reduce hours worked. Perhaps surprisingly, our old welfare system had features that tested both of these predictions. A mother with children received income if she did not work at all, and over a range of earnings, every additional dollar of earnings resulted in a dollar reduction in public support. Against this system that discouraged work, the EITC and Temporary Assistance for Needy Families programs effectively subsidize wages, with the amount of the transfer conditional on the hours of work at low wages. As we expect,

> The available evidence . . . suggests that these programs can increase work and raise income (reduce poverty). These effects appear to be larger in more generous programs. . . . The combination of financial incentives with various types of employment services appears to result in even larger increases in employment and income. . . . The existing evidence is at least suggestive that the combination of financial incentive "carrots" with mandatory job search assistance "sticks" can produce larger employment and income increases than either program by itself.[9]

It should be noted that the substantial increase in labor supply and employment of single mothers that has resulted from the expansion of the EITC and welfare reform is accompanied by a small increase in the labor supply of married men and a decrease in the labor supply of married mothers.[10] Of course, the success of the EITC cannot be judged simply by its effect on labor force participation and employment, but that effect certainly contributes to the bipartisan support for this antipoverty program.

Turning to the effect of income taxes more broadly on work, prediction is more difficult. A marginal income tax rate of 100 percent or more should reduce work effort to zero. An income tax rate of 0 percent should have no effect on work effort. Does work effort decline steadily as the income tax rate increases from 0 percent to 100 percent? While popular discussions of the Laffer curve and other policy paradigms might lead one to expect such a result, theory leads to a more ambiguous conclusion, as we have already discussed. Evidence, too, is inconclusive, but the consensus among econometricians is that the after-tax wage rate has little effect on the labor supply.[11] As this survey has found generally, there is little evidence of strong effects of taxation or tax breaks on hours worked or labor force participation.

CONCLUSIONS

Taxes and tax breaks affect public sector revenues and the distribution of income. They also have the capacity to change behavior. Many changes in the tax code that are pursued by interests for their parochial gain are justified to the citizenry by alleged salutary effects of the tax breaks on behavior. Such claims typically make no attempt to ask why the market economy without the tax break fails to deliver enough of the desired behavior, nor whether the cost of changing behavior is justified by benefits. The public is simply told that through tax break x we get more of the good thing y. When the good thing is saving, investment, and work, we have some evidence on the potency of tax breaks to effect change. This survey suggests that, with a few exceptions—wage subsidies for the very poor, perhaps tax incentives for R&D—claims of broad improvement in incentives to save, invest, and work are, at best, weakly supported by evidence. Incentive effects are difficult to confirm in the data, though many observers continue to believe that they are important.

If aggregate saving, investment, and work effort appear to be insensitive to tax breaks, the allocation of resources among competing saving instruments and investment opportunities is more responsive. Tax breaks do affect the types of assets that savers accumulate and the sectors investors favor. Unfortunately, little evidence is ever offered to suggest why society gains if households own 401k plans rather than other assets, or if the insurance industry grows at the expense of other sectors. Instead, we are asked to believe that tax breaks stimulate total saving or total investment. Such beneficial incentive effects are, at best, undemonstrated.

NOTES

1. Thanks to Eric Toder, Michael Ettlinger, and William Gale for helpful suggestions. Errors remain mine.

2. B. Douglas Bernheim, *Taxation and Saving*, NBER Working Paper 7061, National Bureau of Economic Research, Cambridge, Mass., March 1999.

3. For recent evidence, see James M. Poterba and Arthur A. Samwick, *Taxation and Household Portfolio Composition*, NBER Working Paper 7392, National Bureau of Economic Research, Cambridge, Mass., October 1999.

4. For example, date of birth has been used to identify those most likely to have been drafted into the Vietnam War and those most likely to drop out of high school. Using date of birth as an instrument in statistical analysis has permitted researchers to comment on the effects of military service and education without becoming bogged down in questions of self-selection according to unobservable taste and aptitudes. In studies of saving behavior, such unobservables continue to confound research.

5. Kevin A. Hassett and R. Glenn Hubbard, "Tax Policy and Investment," in A. Auerbach, ed., *Fiscal Policy: Lessons from Economic Research* (Cambridge: MIT Press, 1997).

6. Bronwyn H. Hall and John van Reenen, *How Effective are Fiscal Incentives for R&D?* NBER Working Paper 7098, National Bureau of Economic Research, Cambridge, Mass., April 1999.

7. Jennifer Dunn, *Congressional Record*, July 22, 1999, pp. H6203–04.

8. Leonard Burman, *The Labyrinth of Capital Gains Tax Policy* (Washington, D.C.: The Brookings Institution Press, 1999).

9. Rebecca M. Blank, David Card, and Philip K. Robins, *Financial Incentives for Increasing Work and Income Among Low-Income Families*, NBER Working Paper 6998, National Bureau of Economic Research, Cambridge, Mass., March 1999.

10. See Nada Eissa and Hilary W. Hoynes, *The Earned Income Tax Credit and*

the Labor Supply of Married Couples, NBER Working Paper 6856, National Bureau of Economic Research, Cambridge, Mass., December 1998; and Bruce D. Myers and Dan T. Rosenbaum, *Welfare, the Earned Income Tax Credit, and the Labor Supply of Single Mothers*, NBER Working Paper 7363, National Bureau of Economic Research, Cambridge, Mass., September 1999.

11. James J. Heckman, *What Has Been Learned About Labor Supply in the Past Twenty Years*, American Economic Review, Papers and Proceedings, May 1993.

Our Bucket Is Leaking
Tax Expenditures and Loopholes in the Federal Budget

Michael P. Ettlinger

1

INTRODUCTION

Tax expenditures is the official term used to describe the vast array of government spending programs that are implemented through the Internal Revenue Code—programs that will total $3.4 trillion over the next five years. As the congressional Joint Committee on Taxation (JCT) explains:

> Special income tax provisions are referred to as tax expenditures because they are considered to be analogous to direct outlay programs. . . . Tax expenditures are most similar to those direct spending programs which have no spending limits, and which are available as entitlements to those who meet the statutory criteria established for the programs.[1]

What makes tax expenditures similar to spending programs is that they are special tax provisions that are designed to accomplish some social or economic goal unrelated to equitable tax collection. They are like "entitlements" because they are not subject to annual budget appropriations but are paid out to any business or individual that meets the eligibility rules, regardless of the total cost.

Of the $3.4 trillion in tax expenditures projected over the next five years, $2.94 trillion reduce personal income tax collections and

---

This paper was originally conceived of as an update to "The Hidden Entitlements" by Robert S. McIntyre (Citizens for Tax Justice and the Institute on Taxation and Economic Policy, May 1996) and was written prior to passage of the 2001 bill and does not reflect changes in tax expenditures as a result of that legislation. In addition to updating the original study, the text has been substantially altered to serve the needs of The Century Foundation Working Group on Tax Breaks.

$440 billion reduce corporate income tax collections. This does not represent a clear division between social goals pursued by personal income tax breaks and economic goals pursued by corporate income tax breaks. The corporate portion represents only about a quarter of tax breaks for business and investment. Many tax expenditures in the personal income tax are in support of economic, not purely social, goals. For instance, the $360 billion in tax breaks to individuals for capital gains stands out as a direct subsidy to investors. Direct business tax breaks also reduce personal income tax collections substantially because of the benefits they confer on noncorporate businesses and S-corporations. The tax expenditure for accelerated depreciation in the personal income tax is, to take an example, worth $65 billion over the five years. In addition, substantial tax breaks for pensions, life insurance policies, and other investment vehicles are rationalized on grounds of their positive economic impact. In total, business, investment, and savings subsidies account for half ($1.7 trillion) of all tax expenditures in the corporate and personal income taxes.

Most tax expenditures are regressive, disproportionately benefiting the well-off. One reason for this is the "upside-down" nature of any subsidy that reduces taxable income. Because the personal income tax has graduated rates, the higher the income, the more valuable the reduction in taxable income. To a taxpayer whose income puts them in the 15 percent tax bracket, for example, a reduction in taxable income of $1,000 owing to a tax expenditure is worth $150 in lower tax liability. To a taxpayer in the 36 percent tax bracket, that $1,000 less in taxable income reduces tax by $360. Itemized deductions are an example of an "upside-down" subsidy.

Many tax breaks also disproportionately benefit the wealthy simply because the well-off are much more likely to engage in the subsidized activity. Because capital gains are so heavily concentrated in high-income groups, for example, the benefits of capital gains tax breaks are, not surprisingly, concentrated among those same groups. Capital gains breaks reduce the taxes of those earning more than $200,000 by 2.8 percent of income. The tax reduction for those with incomes below $50,000, however, is negligible.

The most notable exception to the regressive distribution of tax expenditures is the earned income tax credit. This exclusively benefits the lowest income groups—with the greatest benefit going to those with incomes below $20,000.

The existence of substantial tax breaks from the personal and corporate income taxes that predominantly benefit the well-off should not make one forget that the federal income taxes are progressive overall. Characteristics of the tax system other than tax expenditures obviously matter.

Tax expenditures are, however, projected to equal 58 percent of personal and corporate income tax collections over the next five years and are one of the tax system's most important defining features (See Table 1.1, pages 104–105).

The Big Picture

Tax entitlements loom very large in the overall budget picture. The total tax expenditure budget comes to $631 billion in fiscal 2000. That is three times as much as the cost of all means-tested direct spending programs. In fact, it is about 20 percent more than the government spends on defense and interest on the national debt combined.

Because they do not require reappropriation every year, tax expenditures are a favored class of spending. Only those tax expenditures subject to sunset provisions—these are the exception—must be periodically approved by Congress. Also, reductions in tax expenditures are usually treated as tax increases in the legislative arena—not always the most popular choice. Conversely, when new spending is desired, a new tax expenditure is counted as a "tax cut," which is often more appealing than a functionally equivalent "spending increase."

This is not to say that tax expenditures are untouchable. The 1986 Tax Reform Act illustrates this. Because of legislation adopted in 1981, tax expenditures had skyrocketed by 1986. Corporate tax expenditures had reached double the amount of corporate income tax collected—the corporate income tax had become more loophole than tax. Personal income tax expenditures amounted to 85 percent of collections. Provisions such as Individual Retirement Accounts, which had been projected to cost a few hundred million dollars a year, were costing $10 billion annually. Public outrage over no-tax corporations and high-income tax shelters fueled a successful effort to close loopholes and cut rates.

Today, if *all* tax expenditures were eliminated, tax rates could be cut by about 37 percent. If rates were cut uniformly, such a step would, of course, result in an enormous realignment in the tax structure from those who benefit most by the current menu of tax expenditures to those who benefit the least.

CALCULATING TAX EXPENDITURES

By law, the congressional Joint Committee on Taxation and the Treasury Department must issue reports each year listing tax expenditures and their estimated cost.[2] These "tax expenditure budgets" are designed to be informational rather than prescriptive, so

TABLE 1.1
TAX EXPENDITURES, 2000–2004:
SUMMARY COST TABLE
(FISCAL YEARS, $ BILLIONS)

	2000–2004 Corporation	Individual	Total
TOTAL, ALL ITEMS	442.8	2,941.1	3427.4
Total as a % of Income Taxes	47%	59%	58%
BUSINESS & INVESTMENT			
Capital gains (except homes)	5.8	358.3	364.1
Accelerated depreciation	137.1	65.3	202.4
Insurance companies & products	30.3	121.8	152.1
Tax-free bonds, public*	5.8	17.2	117.2
Tax-free bonds, private*	1.6	3.2	24.7
Multinational	86.5	17.1	103.6
Business meals and entertainment	22.5	13.5	36.0
R&D tax breaks	27.7	0.3	27.9
Low-income housing credit	9.6	8.6	18.2
Oil, gas, energy	13.4	2.5	15.9
Timber, agriculture, minerals	2.9	5.7	8.6
Financial institutions (noninsurance)	6.9	—	6.9
Special ESOP rules	4.5	1.3	5.8
Installment sales	1.2	2.7	3.9
Empowerment zones	1.1	1.0	2.0
Other business and investment	53.0	9.6	62.6
Subtotal, business & investment	442.8	665.6	1,151.9
Pensions, Keoghs, IRAs, other savings	—	559.8	559.8
Total, business, investment, and savings	442.8	1,225.4	1,711.7

Totals include benefits enjoyed by state and local governments and nonprofit organizations from lower interest rates.

Table 1.1 (Continued)
Tax Expenditures, 2000–2004:
Summary Cost Table
(Fiscal Years, $ Billions)

	2000–2001 Individuals Only
PERSONAL (NONINVESTMENT)	
Itemized deductions (net)	612.5
Employer-paid health insurance	380.3
Earned Income Tax Credit	157.7
Social Security benefits, etc. (exclusion)	135.6
Child credit	92.4
Other fringe benefits	86.7
Capital gains on homes	81.8
Workmen's compensation, etc.	56.6
Education credits and deductions	42.4
Soldiers and veterans	26.0
Child care credit	11.3
Elderly and blind standard deduction, etc.	10.4
Other personal	22.0
Total, personal	1,715.7
ADDENDUM: ITEMIZED DEDUCTIONS	
Mortgage interest	309.7
S&L taxes (without home property)	207.8
Property taxes (homes)	110.7
Charitable contributions	146.0
Medical expenses	23.8
Casualty losses	1.4
Total, before standard deduction offset	799.3
Net itemized deductions	612.5

Sources: Joint Committee on Taxation, *Estimates of Federal Tax Expenditures for Fiscal Years 2000–2004,* December 22, 1999; Office of Management and Budget, *Budget of the United States Government, Fiscal Year 2001, Analytical Perspectives,* "Tax Expenditures," February 2000; Microsimulation Tax Model, Institute on Taxation and Economic Policy, Washington, D.C., March 2000. Figures are generally averages from the first two sources, except where an item was listed in only one source or one source was based on more current information (or otherwise appeared to be more accurate). Tax-exempt interest benefits were recalculated and reallocated to take account of lower interest rates received by bondholders, benefits to borrowers, and other factors. A few items, such as business meals and entertainment, are not on either list, and were calculated by the Institute on Taxation and Economic Policy. All figures are for fiscal years.

they include almost any tax provision that can plausibly be characterized as the equivalent of a direct spending program.

In some cases, however, an item listed as a tax expenditure may not really be a subsidy. Instead, it might be defensible on pure tax policy grounds as a proper adjustment in computing ability to pay taxes. For example, deductions for state and local income and property taxes are included in the official tax expenditure budgets. Arguably, however, state and local taxes reduce ability to pay federal taxes, and thus deductions for those expenses should not be considered a subsidy. For example, a New York family making $75,000 a year in total income has a lower ability to pay federal taxes than an Arkansas family with the same income because the New York family pays higher state and local taxes. The deduction for extraordinary medical expenses has been defended on similar ability-to-pay grounds, as has the charitable deduction.

These arguments are not universally accepted, however. Taxpayers in states with higher taxes have, through the democratic process, chosen to pay higher taxes in exchange for better government services. Arguably, a federal tax preference for this choice over the alternative is a subsidy that should be counted as a tax expenditure.[3]

Because there is honest disagreement over whether deductions for state and local taxes, large medical costs, and charitable donations are proper adjustments in computing ability to pay taxes or are instead subsidies, they are included in the tax expenditure budget for informational purposes.

Although the rule of thumb is to include in the tax expenditure budget any tax provision that can be construed as a subsidy, there are some items that look remarkably like subsidies but are *not* included on the official tax expenditure lists. For example, the tax code allows a deduction for half of amounts spent on "business meals and entertainment." There is a strong case to be made that this should be counted as a tax expenditure, but it is absent from the official lists.

Despite some controversy at the margins over what should or should not be termed a "tax expenditure," most of the items on the official tax expenditure lists—from mortgage interest deductions to capital gains breaks—are generally agreed to be deviations from normal tax policy that are functionally equivalent to spending programs.

This paper relies heavily on the latest editions of the Treasury and JCT tax expenditure reports, as well as the Institute on Taxation and Economic Policy (ITEP) Microsimulation Tax Model. The ITEP model was used as a "tiebreaker" (along with other data) where JCT and Treasury had differing estimates. In addition, the model is used to show the distributional impact by income level of selected tax expenditure items.[4]

In preparing the tax expenditure lists and summaries, this paper used the Treasury and JCT lists as follows:

- The lists have been consolidated. Treasury and JCT do not always list items in the same way. One list may more finely divide its estimates than the other in a given category. I have tried to aggregate or disaggregate to produce the most useful presentation. I also have organized the lists by somewhat different subject matter than Treasury and JCT.

- Each list contains some items that are not on the other. This partly stems from different assessments of what constitutes a "tax expenditure" in specific cases. In addition, JCT does not report items with a cost of less than $50 million over five years.[5]

- Business meals and entertainment have been added. Also listed, though not included in the totals, are several other tax breaks that are not cited by either Treasury or JCT but that, arguably, are tax expenditures.

- Some tables here have allocated the benefits of tax-exempt bonds differently than is done by JCT and Treasury. The benefits of tax-exempt bonds do not only accrue to the taxpayer who holds the bonds. State and local governments pay lower rates on their borrowing by virtue of the tax exemption. Private organizations that borrow through tax-exempt bonds also benefit. On the other hand, purchasers of tax-exempt instruments do not get a benefit equal to the amount they would pay in tax were the same bonds taxable. If the bonds were not tax-exempt, the bond purchasers would receive higher interest payments. So the net benefit is less than the reduced tax. In some of the tables the benefits of tax-exempt bonds are measured accounting for these considerations.

- In some instances where the estimates were significantly different, either the Treasury or JCT estimate was chosen over that of the other agency. To do this, I used independent data sources and the

ITEP model to assess the relative merits of the two estimates. I also looked to see which agency has revisited its estimate most recently. Although the tax expenditure reports come out annually, it is apparent that significant reestimation does not occur every year for every tax expenditure. When reestimation does occur, there is sometimes a significant adjustment from one year's estimate to the next that does not reflect a change in tax policy or taxpayer behavior. The adjustment can reflect a more sophisticated estimate. This paper takes into consideration which agency has most recently reexamined its estimates.

- Many of the Treasury and JCT estimates differ from each other for no discernible reason. In those cases, where there is no basis to choose between them, they have been averaged.

- A tax expenditure has been calculated for *total* itemized deductions. Treasury and JCT report tax expenditure amounts for each itemized deduction separately. But because of their interaction with the standard deduction, the sum of these separate amounts overstates the total cost of itemized deductions. The additional calculation presented here rectifies this.

An issue often raised with tax expenditure reports is whether the amounts listed actually reflect potential budget savings were the tax expenditure provisions to be eliminated. Although less frequently raised, the same question could be asked of ordinary expenditure budgets. Line items in expenditure budgets, in general, do not accurately reflect the budget savings to be gained by abolishing specific programs or groups of programs. Eliminating all veterans benefits would, for example, reduce the federal budget by less than the amount currently spent on those programs because spending would increase in food stamps, Medicaid, and other entitlement programs. Eliminating the State Department would presumably lead to behavioral changes around the world that would result in increased military spending. Not to mention that certain of the department's activities would undoubtedly be taken up by other agencies.[6]

Similarly, line items in the tax expenditure budget do not necessarily reflect the amount of revenue that would be raised by repeal of each provision. Proper revenue estimates would require consideration of taxpayer behavior and the interactions among tax expenditures. One cannot, however, make a general statement that accounting for these concerns would result in revenue estimates that are higher, or lower, than the amounts reported in the tax expenditure budgets.

In the case of taxpayer behavior, repeal of a given tax expenditure may cause a shift to more heavily subsidized, less subsidized, or equally subsidized behavior. Take the example of the research and experimentation tax credit. If the credit were repealed, some companies would presumably engage in less research and experimentation. Of those companies, some would divert funds formerly used for science to paying dividends. Revenue from those companies would increase *more* than the amount of the credit they had been receiving because, in addition to losing the credit, the companies would lose the deductions for the expenses previously incurred in research and experimentation. Other companies, however, would divert spending from research and experimentation to another tax-favored activity (low-income housing, perhaps). For those companies, the net revenue gain from repealing the credit would be *less* than the amount of the credit they had been receiving. Using the tax expenditure amount as an estimate of the revenue to be gained from repealing the credit implicitly assumes the changes in behavior balance out—that the revenue impact is what it would be if all companies persisted with the same amount of research and experimentation as with the credit extant.

A problem with adding together tax expenditure amounts to estimate the revenue to be gained by their repeal is that tax expenditures interact. The revenue to be gained from repealing several exclusions from income could be *more* than the sum of the parts. Repealing exclusions raises taxable income and puts taxpayers into higher-rate tax brackets. The more exclusions that are repealed at once, the more taxpayers find themselves facing higher tax brackets and the greater the revenue yield of repeal.

Itemized deductions are the most clear-cut, and significant, example of a group of tax expenditures adding up to a greater amount than their combined repeal would raise in revenue because of interations. This is the one group of tax expenditures for which the tabulations used here have accounted for the interactions. Other than with itemized deductions, this paper has not attempted to resolve the ambiguity as to whether tax expenditure amounts listed overstate or understate the revenue that would be expected on repeal.

2

TAX EXPENDITURES FOR BUSINESS, INVESTMENT, AND SAVINGS

Over the 2000–2004 period, almost precisely half of all tax expenditures, $1.7 trillion, are expected to go to subsidize business, investment, and savings (see Table 2.1, page 112). The $226 billion for business, savings, and investment subsidies for individuals in 2000 actually exceeded the total amount of personal savings for the year.

One of the principal goals of the 1986 Tax Reform Act was to curb the harmful economic distortions that the "supply-side" tax-expenditure-based policies of the 1970s and early 1980s had produced. As the official report on the 1986 act notes, in that era "the output attainable from our capital resources was reduced because too much investment occurred in tax-favored sectors and too little investment occurred in sectors that were more productive but which were tax-disadvantaged."[1]

Although the 1986 reform bill did not eliminate all tax-induced investment distortions, it did make great progress. There has, however, been significant backsliding over the past fifteen years.

CAPITAL GAINS

Capital gains are profits reflecting increased values of stocks, bonds, investment real estate, and other "capital assets." Tax expenditures favoring the predominantly well-off recipients of capital gains income were greatly expanded in 1997. Total current capital gains

TABLE 2.1
BUSINESS, INVESTMENT, AND
SAVINGS TAX EXPENDITURES:
CORPORATIONS AND INDIVIDUALS, 2000–2004
($ BILLIONS)

Capital gains (except homes)	364.1
Accelerated depreciation	202.4
Insurance companies and products	152.1
Tax-free bonds, public (with state and local savings)	117.2
Tax-free bonds, private (with nonprofit savings)	24.7
Multinational tax breaks	103.6
Business meals and entertainment	36.0
R&E tax breaks	27.9
Low-income housing credit	18.2
Oil, gas, energy	15.9
Timber, agriculture, minerals	8.6
Financial institutions (noninsurance)	6.9
Special ESOP rules	5.8
Installment sales	3.9
Empowerment zones	2.0
Other business and investment	62.6
Pensions, Keoghs, IRAs	558.5
Other individual savings incentives	1.3
TOTAL	1,711.7

Source: Same as Table 1.1.

tax expenditures (excluding those related to homes) are estimated to cost $364 billion over the next five years (see Table 2.2).

Capital gains are not taxed at all unless and until they are "realized"—generally on sale of an appreciated asset. And, even when gains are realized, individuals pay lower tax rates on capital gains than on so-called ordinary income.

As a result, investment vehicles are often designed to maximize the share of profits that are in the form of capital gains—both realized and unrealized. Indeed, on individual tax returns, total realized capital gains are more than double stock dividends (though not all of

TABLE 2.2
CAPITAL GAINS (EXCEPT HOMES),
2000–2004 ($ BILLIONS)

Lower rates on capital gains income	207.2
Exclusion of capital gains on inherited property	141.6
Deferral on "like-kind exchanges"	7.8
Carryover basis of capital gains on gifts	7.4
Deferral of gain in disaster areas	0.1
TOTAL	364.1

Source: Same as for Table 1.1.

the discrepancy is attributable to the structuring of investments, as significant capital gains are realized on assets other than stock; see Table 2.3, page 114).

This is not to say that capital gains are common for most taxpayers. In fact, only about 14 percent of taxpayers report any capital gains at all. For those with incomes in excess of $200,000, however, about two-thirds report capital gains each year. This top income group, representing 2.6 percent of families and individuals, accounts for more than 70 percent of reported capital gains realizations.

Investment income of any sort is a greater proportion of income at higher income levels. But even among different sources of investment income, capital gains is exceptionally skewed toward the high end. Dividends and interest, are a greater share of unearned income for lower- and middle-income families than capital gains but a smaller portion at the top.

Proponents of low capital gains tax rates argue that the cost of capital gains tax breaks is much less than first appears. A surge in capital gains after 1978 and 1981 rate cuts, they contend, proves that capital gains tax cuts cause the well-off to cash in far more unrealized gains, thereby mitigating or even eliminating the apparent revenue loss from a lowered capital gains tax. To be sure, reported gains (before exclusion) did increase rapidly in the late 1970s and early 1980s. In nominal terms, they rose from $45 billion in 1977 to $80 billion in 1980 to $176 billion by 1985. Adjusted for the growth of the economy, this represented a 90 percent increase in reported gains from 1977 to 1985. Even if *all* the increase

TABLE 2.3
AVERAGE CAPITAL GAINS,
DIVIDENDS, AND INTEREST IN 1999

Income Group	Capital Gains	Dividends	Interest
$0–10,000	33	35	149
$10–20,000	86	117	348
$20–30,000	177	242	670
$30–40,000	375	476	1,045
$40–50,000	449	550	1,387
$50–75,000	1,040	834	1,690
$75–100,000	2,518	1,538	2,887
$100–200,000	6,377	3,634	5,496
$200,000+	110,023	26,025	32,545
ALL FAMILIES	$3,202	$1,180	$ 1,932

Source: Microsimulation Tax Model, Institute on Taxation and Economic Policy, Washington D.C., March 2000.

in capital gains realizations could somehow be attributed to the tax cuts, though, these figures would still indicate that the tax cuts lowered revenues since the capital gains tax rate was cut about in half between 1977 and 1985. But much of the increase in reported gains simply reflected the stock market's recovery from the oil-price shocks of the 1970s—and thus would have happened even absent the tax changes.

Moreover, a very large share of the increased capital gains in the first half of the 1980s probably represented tax shelter conversions of ordinary income into gains. A surge in reported gains that reflects tax sheltering is actually evidence of revenue loss associated with a capital gains rate reduction, not an offsetting revenue gain.

So do lower tax rates on capital gains cause people to cash in more gains than they otherwise would have (not counting tax shelter effects)? The answer is probably yes, but the long-term magnitude of such induced realizations would figure to be quite low. A study by Congressional Budget Office economists Leonard Burman and William

Randolph compared capital gains realizations by a sample of taxpayers over time. They found large transitory effects when a taxpayer's individual circumstances changed and when the federal government made major revisions in capital gains taxation.[2] But, on a long-term basis, the study found very little correlation between the tax code's treatment of capital gains and levels of realizations. In fact, the study found that "the permanent elasticity is not significantly different from zero."[3]

Twenty percent maximum rate. The 1986 Tax Reform Act set tax rates on realized capital gains at the same rates as on wages, dividends, and other income. (Previously, realized capital gains had been 60 percent tax-exempt.) But in 1990, Congress reinstated a small preference by capping the capital gains rate at 28 percent while setting the top regular income tax rate at 31 percent. In the 1993 budget bill, this capital gains preference was greatly expanded to provide what amounted to a 30 percent capital gains exclusion for top-bracket taxpayers (the difference between the new 39.6 percent top regular tax rate and the continuing 28 percent maximum capital gains rate).

As part of the 1997 tax act, capital gains rates were reduced to their pre-1986 top rate of 20 percent. In addition, a top capital gains rate of 10 percent was put in place for those in the 15 percent ordinary income bracket.

The benefits of these lower rates, not surprisingly, go disproportionately to those with the most capital gains—the well-off. Eighty-seven percent of the tax savings from the current special capital gains tax rates for individuals, goes to the best-off 2.6 percent of all families—those with annual incomes in excess of $200,000 (see Table 2.4, page 116).

The rates are scheduled to go down further for property held five years or more. The top rate for such property *acquired* after 2000 is18 percent. For those in the 15 percent ordinary income bracket, the capital gains rate drops to 8 percent for property *sold* after 2000 that has been held for five years or more.

Lower capital gains rates extended to normal business profits. Historically, favorable capital gains treatment has normally been limited to profits from the sale of investments (stocks, bonds, etc.). But several industries have succeeded in getting part of their normal business profits treated as capital gains. Special capital gains treatment is currently available for sales of timber by individuals, for coal and iron ore, and for certain agricultural income.

TABLE 2.4
BENEFITS OF CURRENT LAW'S SPECIAL LOWER
RATES ON CAPITAL GAINS IN 1999

Income Group ($-000)	% with Capital Gains	% of All Capital Gains	Average Tax Break (all returns)	Tax Break as % of Income	% of Total Tax Break
$0–10	2.2	0.1	$0	0.0	0.0
$10–20	3.8	0.5	$2	0.0	0.1
$20–30	7.3	0.9	$5	0.0	0.2
$30–40	11.8	1.4	$12	0.0	0.4
$40–50	15.9	1.3	$20	0.0	0.5
$50–75	20.8	4.8	$57	0.1	2.2
$75–100	33.0	5.3	$161	0.2	2.8
$100–200	45.7	12.3	$451	0.3	7.2
$200+	64.4	73.1	$15,866	2.8	86.7
ALL	14.6	100.0	$389	0.8	100.0

Source: Microsimulation Tax Model, Institute on Taxation and Economic Policy, Washington, D.C., March 2000.

Deferral and capital gains tax breaks for gifts and inheritances. Capital gains are not taxed until assets are actually sold. As a result, investors can put off tax on their gains indefinitely. (They also can avoid tax on realized gains by selectively realizing losses on other investments in the same year.) This deferral is unavailable, of course, for other kinds of income such as savings account interest—even if the money is left in the bank. Multibillionaire Warren Buffett, for example, has structured his investment company so that it has not paid a dividend since 1966. Instead, Buffett's $14 billion or so in accrued capital gains remains unrealized and thus untaxed.

Deferral does not, however, preclude investor use of the cash value of the investments held. Owners of investment assets that have gone up in value can cash in their capital gains without tax by borrowing against the appreciation. Refinancing is an enormous tax shelter for, among others, real estate speculators.

When an asset holder gives away property, the deferral is transferred to the recipient. The recipient takes over the giver's "basis" in the donated property—generally the cost when the property was first acquired. That carryover of basis—instead of taxing the gain—allows a continued deferral of unrealized capital gains.

When an asset holder dies, deferral turns into waiver. Heirs pay no tax on capital gains that accrued prior to the time they inherit. Technically this is accomplished by "stepping up" the basis of the inherited property to its value at the time it is inherited.

Deferral, and particularly stepped-up basis at death, create a very strong incentive for the owners of capital assets to hold onto their property.

The value of deferral in an asset holder's lifetime, including the benefits of refinancing, is not counted by Treasury or JCT as a tax expenditure and is not included in the lists presented here. The costs of continued deferral for the recipients of gifts and "stepped-up-basis" at death are included.

Indefinite tax deferral for "like-kind exchanges" of real estate. Normally, when someone sells appreciated property he or she must pay tax on the capital gain. But someone who sells rental real estate and purchases other rental property can put off paying capital gains taxes on the sale indefinitely by characterizing the transaction as an "exchange" of properties with another investor.

ACCELERATED DEPRECIATION

Accelerated depreciation now is the largest of all business tax loopholes. It will cost $202 billion over the next five years (see Table 2.5, page 118). Of that, $137 billion will go to corporations and $65 billion to individuals.

Accelerated depreciation lets businesses write off the costs of their machinery and buildings faster than they actually wear out. In practice, that means sharply lower tax bills for corporations and individuals that can take advantage of the tax breaks.

The 1981 tax legislation hugely expanded accelerated depreciation and other corporate tax breaks—most notably the investment tax credit. By 1983, studies found that half of the largest and most profitable companies in the nation had paid no federal income tax at all in at least one of the years the depreciation changes had been in effect. More than a quarter of 250 well-known companies paid nothing at all

TABLE 2.5
ACCELERATED DEPRECIATION, 2000–2004
($ BILLIONS)

Accelerated depreciation of machinery and equipment	157.4
Accelerated depreciation on rental housing	27.2
Accelerated department of buildings.except rental housing	8.3
Expensing of certain small-equipment investments	6.2
Tax incentives for preserving historic structures	1.8
Amortization of business start-up costs	1.4
Expensing costs of removing architectural barriers	0.0
TOTAL	202.4

Source: Same as Table 1.1.

in the three-year period from 1981 to 1983, despite $50 billion in pre-tax U.S. profits. This sort of rampant tax avoidance persisted through 1986.[4]

The 1986 act repealed the investment tax credit and sharply reduced depreciation writeoffs for buildings. The changes greatly scaled back corporate tax avoidance opportunities and made taxpayers out of most of the companies that had been able to avoid taxes in the early 1980s.

Notwithstanding predictions that investment would plummet without the subsidies, business investment flourished. Real business investment grew by 2.7 percent a year from 1986 to 1989. That compared favorably with the 1.9 percent growth rate from 1981 to 1986. Even more significant, while tax-preference-induced construction of office buildings tapered off after reform, business investment in industrial machinery and plants boomed. As money flowed out of tax shelters, industrial investment jumped by 5.1 percent a year from 1986 to 1989, after actually falling at a 2 percent annual rate from 1981 to 1986. As former Reagan Treasury official J. Gregory Ballentine told *Business Week,* "It's very difficult to find much relationship between [corporate tax breaks] and investment. In 1981 manufacturing had its largest tax cut ever and immediately went down the tubes. In 1986 they had their largest tax increase and went gangbusters [on investment]."[5]

Despite its advances, the 1986 Tax Reform Act did not end the preference for corporate depreciation. Businesses still write off the cost of their machinery and equipment considerably faster than it actually wears out. This remaining tax break has proved much more expensive than originally anticipated by the drafters of the 1986 Tax Reform Act. Like any tax concession targeted to corporations, accelerated depreciation is primarily a benefit to the very well-off (who own the lion's share of corporate stock and other capital).

Today's depreciation rules reduce the effective tax rate on the profits from typical investments in machinery to about half the statutory 35 percent rate. One can see examples of that effect by a quick perusal of corporate annual reports. For example, in 1995, Eastman Kodak paid an effective federal tax rate of only 17.3 percent—less than half the 35 percent statutory corporate tax rate— mainly because of $124 million in tax relief from accelerated depreciation.

Economists also complain that accelerated depreciation often skews investment decisions away from what makes the most business sense and toward tax-sheltering activities. This can favor short-term, tax-motivated investments over long-term investments.

One of the claims in support of accelerated depreciation is that without it depreciation would be understated because it would ignore the impact on asset values of inflation. At recent, low levels of inflation, however, depreciation is still overstated. Moreover, when equipment is purchased with borrowed money, the current tax system produces outright "negative" tax rates—making such investments more profitable after tax than before tax because depreciation is accelerated but there is no adjustment for inflation in the taking of interest deductions on the loans. A negative tax rate does not do a company any more good than a zero tax rate in a given year. As a result, corporate buying and selling of excess tax breaks through equipment "leasing" deals has remained widespread.

- General Electric, for example, avoided a total of $1 billion in federal income taxes from 1986 to 1992 attributable to activities of its leasing subsidiary, GE Capital Services.[6]

- From 1980 to 1992, total corporate leasing deductions rose from $92 billion to $196 billion in constant 1992 dollars—an increase of 114 percent (compared to a 45 percent rise in total corporate receipts).[7]

In general, the law has become more favorable to accelerated depreciation since 1986. The changes have not, however, come as a result of the rules directly governing accelerated depreciation under the ordinary income tax. Instead, relaxed alternative minimum tax rules have been the culprit.

The purpose of the alternative minimum tax (AMT) is to ensure that corporations and individuals with substantial incomes must pay significant income tax even if they take advantage of large amounts in tax preferences. The AMT disallows many tax preferences but is imposed at lower rates than the regular income tax. Taxpayers must pay the greater of the AMT or the regular income tax. The vast majority of taxpayers are not affected, but those with substantial incomes who shelter most of their income from regular taxation may owe the AMT.

For corporations, the most significant tax preference the AMT limited was accelerated depreciation. The AMT was designed to address indirectly the problem of negative tax rates for debt-financed purchases of equipment by lowering depreciation deductions for heavily leveraged companies.

In the 1993 tax act, however, the rules for recalculating depreciation under the AMT were greatly relaxed, and in 1997 the AMT's limits on accelerated depreciation were repealed. Relaxing of the AMT has undoubtedly permitted many companies to take greater advantage of accelerated depreciation and has greatly reduced their taxes.

EXPENSING

A key feature of various "flat tax" and other proposals is "expensing" of capital expenditures. Expensing is very accelerated depreciation, allowing the entire cost to be written off immediately no matter how long the asset will be contributing to profits. The stated goal is to reduce the effective tax rate on profits from new corporate investment to zero. Under current law, expensing is allowed up to a maximum, in 2000, of $20,000 per investment (with a total maximum per taxpayer of about $200,000).

TAX BREAKS FOR MULTINATIONAL CORPORATIONS

Multinational corporations, whether American- or foreign-owned, are supposed to pay taxes on the profits they earn in the United States. In addition, American companies and individuals are not supposed to gain tax advantages from moving their operations or investments to off-shore "tax havens." But our tax laws often fail to achieve these goals.

The primary ways that multinational corporations avoid taxation have not, however, generally been defined as "tax expenditures." This is because the problems in our taxation of multinational companies stem mainly from the inherent difficulty in enforcing the rules we use to try to determine how much of a corporation's worldwide earnings relate to its U.S. activities and therefore are subject to U.S. tax. In essence, the IRS must try to scrutinize every movement of goods and services between a multinational company's domestic and foreign operations and then attempt to assure that a fair, arm's length "transfer price" was assigned (on paper) to each real or notional transaction. If the IRS could do this, the approach would work.

But companies have a huge incentive to pretend that their American operations pay too much or charge too little to their foreign operations for goods and services (for tax purposes only), thereby minimizing their U.S. taxable income. In other words, companies try to set their "transfer prices" to shift income *away* from the United States and shift deductible expenses *into* the United States.

* Say a big American company has $10 billion in total sales—half in the United States and half in Germany—and $8 billion in total expenses—again half and half. With $1 billion in actual U.S. profits and a 35 percent tax rate, the company ought to pay $350 million in U.S. income taxes. But suppose that, for U.S. tax purposes, the company is able to treat five-eighths of its expenses—or $5 billion—as U.S.-related. That leaves it with zero U.S. taxable profit. Although our tax system has rules to mitigate this kind of abuse, companies still have plenty of room to maneuver.

* Here is a real-world example: In its 1987 annual report to its stockholders, IBM said that a third of its worldwide profits were earned by its U.S. operations. But on its federal tax return, IBM treated so much of its research and development expenses as

U.S.-related that it reported almost no American earnings—despite $25 billion in U.S. sales that year. As a result, IBM's federal income taxes for 1987 were virtually wiped out.[8]

• A few years ago, Intel won a case in the tax court letting it treat millions of dollars in profits from selling U.S.-made computer chips as Japanese income for U.S. tax purposes—and therefore exempt from U.S. tax—even though a tax treaty between the U.S. and Japan requires Japan to treat the profits as American—and therefore exempt from Japanese tax. As too often happens, the profits thus became "nowhere income"—not taxable anywhere.[9]

A May 1992 Congressional Budget Office report found that "increasingly aggressive transfer pricing by . . . multinational corporations" may be one source of the shortfall in corporate tax payments in recent years compared to what was predicted after the 1986 corporate tax reforms.[10]

The official list of tax expenditures in the international area—totaling $104 billion over the next five years (see Table 2.6)—focuses on special rules to permit companies to allocate more of their income to foreign countries for U.S. tax purposes than would otherwise be allowed. Thus, the list includes items such as:

TABLE 2.6
MULTINATIONAL TAX BREAKS, 2000–2004
($ BILLIONS)

Deferral of income from controlled foreign corporations	27.5
Inventory property sales source rules exception	22.0
Exclusion of income of Foreign Sales Corporations	19.0
Exclusion of income earned abroad by U.S. citizens	17.1
Possessions tax credit	15.3
Interest allocation rules for certain financial operation	2.4
Deferral of tax on shipping companies	0.3
TOTAL	$103.6

Source: Same as Table 1.1.

- Indefinite "deferral" of tax on the profits of controlled foreign subsidiaries. Tax is not paid until the profits are repatriated to the United States—if they ever are.

- "Source" rules that treat certain kinds of U.S. profits as foreign. These rules primarily benefit U.S. exporters.

- The "possessions tax credit," which greatly reduces tax on investments in Puerto Rico and other U.S. possessions. (This credit has been cut and is being phased down.)

- Exclusion of income earned abroad by U.S. citizens. This is justified as an encouragement to citizens to work abroad to promote American exports. It is not, however, targeted to individuals so employed.

These tax expenditures are, however, the tip of the iceberg. Some have estimated that the current system is leaking an additional, approximately equal amount through "transfer pricing" abuses. Arguably this is an enforcement problem, not a tax expenditure issue. But using an inherently unenforceable mechanism for calculating the taxes of multinational corporations is as effective in subsidizing their activities as would be an explicit, statutory, tax break.

INTEREST EARNED BY FOREIGNERS

Also not listed in the official tax expenditure budget but a major tax break nonetheless is the tax exemption for interest earned in the United States by foreigners. Such interest (on loans to American companies and the U.S. government) was exempted from U.S. taxation in 1984. This interest income is not reported to foreigners' home governments, and tax evasion is said to be the norm. As a result, the United States has become a major international tax haven. There is evidence that not only foreign tax cheats but also Americans posing as foreigners have been taking advantage of this loophole. Reinstating the tax has been proposed, with a waiver of the tax if a foreign lender supplies the information necessary to report the interest income to the lender's home government.

TAX-EXEMPT BONDS

Individuals and corporations that lend money to states and localities pay no federal income tax on the interest they earn. This allows states and cities to pay reduced interest rates. But the money that state and local governments save in lower interest payments is considerably less than the cost of the tax break to the federal government—which is expected to be $142 billion over the next five years (see Table 2.7).

Recently, interest rates on long-term state and local tax-exempt bonds have averaged about 5.8 percent. That is about 15 percent lower than the taxable interest paid on comparable Treasury and corporate bonds, which pay about 6.9 percent.[11] Most interest on state and local bonds, however, goes to lenders in federal tax brackets considerably higher than 15 percent. In fact, since about a quarter of the tax breaks for tax-exempt bonds go to 35 percent

TABLE 2.7
TAX-EXEMPT BONDS, 2000–2004
($ BILLIONS)

Tax-free bonds, public (with state and local savings)	117.2
Tax-free bonds, private (with nonprofit savings)	24.7
Private nonprofit health facility bonds	6.3
Mortgage subsidy bonds	4.7
Airports, docks, sports and convention facilities bonds	3.7
Private, nonprofit educational facility bonds	3.0
Pollution control, sewage and waste disposal facilities	2.4
Small-issue industrial development bonds	1.6
Student loan bonds	1.3
Rental housing bonds	0.8
Energy facility bonds	0.6
Credit for holders of zone academy bonds	0.2
Veterans housing bonds	0.2
TOTAL	141.9

Source: Same as Table 1.1.

bracket corporations (banks and so forth), and 84 percent of the remaining tax subsidies go to individual taxpayers making more than $100,000, about two-thirds of the federal subsidy ends up as a windfall to well-off investors.

- For example, a very high income, top-bracket individual would pay about $40,800 in federal taxes on $100,000 in interest earned from investing in taxable bonds. But if the person invests in tax-exempt bonds instead, the federal government loses the $40,800, while the state or local government issuing the bond saves only $15,200 in reduced interest expense. The remaining benefit from the tax subsidy goes straight to the wealthy investor.

- Likewise, a bank or other 35 percent bracket corporation that earns $100,000 in tax-exempt interest gets a federal tax subsidy equal to $35,000. Since the local government saves only $15,200 on the interest it pays, however, the bank's windfall is equal to almost $20,000—almost 60 percent of the cost of the subsidy to the federal government.

Why is the market for tax-exempt bonds so inefficient? The apparent reason is that, while most tax-free bonds are held by high-bracket individuals and corporations, on the margin, states and localities find it necessary to make their bonds attractive to taxpayers in lower brackets. In addition, because the subsidy is tax-bracket dependent, states, to attract buyers for their bonds, have to protect bondholders from the *possibility* of falling into a lower bracket in a given year.

In addition to bonds sold by state and local governments to finance government projects, under many circumstances private companies and individuals can "borrow" the ability to issue tax-free bonds from state and local governments. States and cities have extended the right to borrow tax-free to businesses building airports, rental housing, and electric plants and to individuals taking out mortgages and student loans and borrowing for other purposes. Indeed, before reforms in the mid-1980s, there was almost no limit on what states could authorize tax-exempt financing for—and since the federal government was picking up the bill, there was no internal fiscal constraint on the states. Reforms now generally limit the total amount of such private use of tax-free financing—through a state-by-state volume cap—but it still remains a major drain on the federal Treasury. In fact, $25 billion, or more than a fifth of the $142 billion total tax expenditure for tax-exempt bonds over the next five years, stems from tax-free, nongovernmental bonds used to finance private projects.

Overall, I calculate that only 29 percent of the total subsidy for tax-exempt bonds goes to state and local governments in the form of lower interest rates on their public purpose borrowing. Forty-two percent of the tax subsidy goes to individual lenders and borrowers, 27 percent to corporate lenders and borrowers, and the remaining 26 percent to nonprofit hospitals and schools (see Table 2.8). Direct federal subsidies to state and local governments would obviously be more efficient.

Because the tax exemption for bonds has the "upside-down" effect described earlier, and because better-off taxpayers invest a larger portion of their income, this tax expenditure is far more beneficial to the well-off. Including both personal and corporate windfalls, more than 80 percent of the tax break goes to those with incomes in excess of $100,000 (see Table 2.9).

TABLE 2.8
WHERE FEDERAL SUBSIDIES
FOR TAX-EXEMPT BONDS GO

INTEREST SAVINGS FOR BORROWERS:	
State and local governments	29%
Individual borrowers*	2%
Corporate borrowers**	2%
Nonprofit hospitals and schools	2%
WINDFALL RETURNS TO LENDERS:	
Individual bondholders	40%
Corporate bondholders	25%
TOTAL	100%

*Includes savings on housing subsidy bonds (with mortgage credit certificates) and student loan bonds.
**Includes interest savings on other private purpose bonds except benefits to nonprofit hospitals and schools.

TABLE 2.9
TAX BREAKS FROM TAX-EXEMPT BONDS

Income Group ($-000)	Average Tax Benefit (all families)	Benefit as a % of Income	% of Total Tax Benefit
$0–10	3	0.1	0.3
$10–20	7	0.0	1.0
$20–30	14	0.1	1.6
$30–40	22	0.1	1.8
$40–50	32	0.1	2.0
$50–75	59	0.1	5.9
$75–100	133	0.2	6.2
$100–200	413	0.3	17.5
$200+	4,360	0.8	63.6
ALL	$146	0.3%	100.0%

Note: Tax benefits include personal and corporate income tax savings and corporate interest savings, net of reduced personal and corporate interest received. They exclude benefits from lower interest paid by state and local governments, nonprofit organizations, and individuals.

Source: Microsimulation Tax Model, Institute on Taxation and Economic Policy, Washington, D.C., March 2000.

INSURANCE COMPANIES AND PRODUCTS

Insurance companies enjoy a wealth of federal tax breaks, both at the corporate level and for their customers. In total, these tax expenditures are expected to cost $152 billion over the next five years (see Table 2.10, page 128). The tax subsidies include:

Interest on life insurance savings. Interest and other investment income earned on accumulated life insurance premiums are not taxed either as they accrue or when they are received by beneficiaries upon the death of the insured.

Deduction of unpaid property loss reserves of property and casualty companies. Property and casualty insurance companies can deduct not only

TABLE 2.10
INSURANCE COMPANIES AND PRODUCTS, 2000–2004
($ BILLIONS)

Exclusion of interest on life insurance savings	128.7
Deduction of unpaid loss reserves for property and casualty companies	14.7
Special treatment of life insurance company reserves	6.1
Exemption for ins. comps. owned by tax-exempt organizations	1.2
Special deduction for Blue Cross/Blue Shield companies	0.8
Small life insurance company deduction	0.5
Special alternative tax on small property and causality companies	0.0
TOTAL	$152.1

Source: Same as Table 1.1.

claims paid but also the discounted value of anticipated claims on current policies that they assert will have to be paid.

Special treatment of life insurance company reserves. Likewise, life insurance companies can deduct "reserves" that exceed claims actually paid. Insurance companies also are not taxed on investment income stemming from so-called structured settlement amounts.

Insurance companies owned by tax-exempt organizations and Blue Cross and Blue Shield. Generally, the income earned by life and property and casualty insurance companies is subject to tax, even if special rules apply. Insurance operations conducted by fraternal societies and "voluntary employee benefit associations," however, are tax-exempt. Some of the leading "nonprofit" fraternal society insurers write tens of billions of dollars in insurance coverage—and are quite lucrative for their senior employees.

Although Blue Cross and Blue Shield do not qualify as tax-exempt charities and are largely indistinguishable in the products they offer from other insurance companies, they get exceptions from normal insurance company income tax accounting rules that effectively eliminate all their taxes. This appears to be in recognition of their past tax-exempt status and their continuing (though varying) community activities.

OIL, GAS, AND ENERGY TAX BREAKS

Oil and gas companies receive substantial subsidies to encourage domestic production. Although it has devised these incentives for producers, Congress also has provided subsidies designed to reduce oil and gas consumption through use of alternative fuels and conservation. In total, the apparently conflicting tax breaks for oil, gas, and energy are expected to cost $16 billion over the next five years (see Table 2.11). Oil, gas, and energy tax breaks include:

Percentage depletion. Independent oil and gas (and other fuel mineral) producers are generally allowed to take "percentage depletion" deductions rather than writing off actual costs over the productive life of the property based on the fraction of the resource extracted. Since percentage depletion deductions are simply a flat percentage of gross revenues, unlike depreciation or cost depletion, they can greatly exceed actual costs. Percentage depletion rates are 22 percent of gross income for uranium, 15 percent for oil, gas, and oil shale, and 10 percent for coal. The deduction is limited to half of the net income from a property, except for oil and gas, where the deduction can be

TABLE 2.11
OIL, GAS, AND ENERGY, 2000–2004
($ BILLIONS)

Alternative fuel production credit	5.1
Oil, gas, and other fuels percentage depletion	3.3
Gasohol excise tax exemption and credit	3.3
Expensing of intangible drilling costs	1.2
Enhanced oil recovery costs credit	1.0
Special tax rate for nuclear dicommissioning reserve fund	0.8
New technology credit	0.6
Tax breaks for "clean-fuel" vehicles and properties	0.4
Exclusion of conservation subsidies from utilities	0.3
TOTAL	15.9

Source: Same as Table 1.1

100 percent. Production from geothermal deposits is eligible for percentage depletion at 65 percent of net income.

Exploration and development costs. Normally, businesses can write off their investments only as the value of those investments diminishes. Oil companies, however, can write off their "intangible drilling costs," that is, much of their investments in finding and developing domestic oil and gas wells, immediately, even for successful wells.[12] (Major, integrated oil companies can immediately deduct only 70 percent of such investments and must write off the remaining 30 percent over five years.) A similar tax break is granted for the costs of surface stripping and the construction of shafts and tunnels for other fuel minerals.

Oil and gas exception to passive loss limitation. Although owners of working interests in oil and gas properties are subject to the alternative minimum tax, they are exempted from the "passive income" limitations. This means that the "working interest-holder," who manages on behalf of himself and all other owners the development of wells and incurs all the costs of their operation, may use oil and gas tax losses to shelter income from other sources.

Alternative fuel production and new technology credits. A credit of three dollars per barrel (in 1979 dollars) of oil-equivalent production is provided for several forms of "alternative fuels." (It is available as long as the price of oil stays below $29.50 in 1979 dollars.) Alternative fuels include shale oil, natural gas produced from hard-to-access places and garbage, and synthetic oil and gas produced from coal. Also, a credit of 1.5 cents is provided per kilowatt hour of electricity produced from renewable resources such as wind, biomass, and chicken waste. A 10 percent credit is available for investment in solar and geothermal energy facilities. These credits are scheduled to expire in 2002.

Alcohol fuel credit. Manufacturers of gasohol (a motor fuel composed of 10 percent alcohol) get a tax subsidy of fifty-four cents per gallon of alcohol used in 2000 (it phases down to fifty-one cents by 2005).[13] This enormous subsidy has yielded big profits for Archer Daniels Midland, the nation's chief gasohol producer.

TIMBER, AGRICULTURE, MINERALS

Timber, agriculture, and mineral extraction have long been favored by the tax code over other industries. These tax expenditures are expected to reduced federal revenues by $8.6 billion from 2000 through 2004 (see Table 2.12). Besides the capital gains breaks that apply to such businesses, these tax expenditures include:

Exploration and development costs. As is true for fuel minerals, certain capital outlays associated with exploration and development of nonfuel minerals may be written off immediately rather than depreciated over the life of the asset.

Percentage depletion. Most nonfuel mineral extractors also make use of percentage depletion rather than cost depletion, with percentage depletion rates ranging from 22 percent for sulfur down to 5 percent for sand and gravel.

TABLE 2.12
TIMBER, AGRICULTURE, MINERALS, 2000–2004
($ BILLIONS)

Cash accounting for agriculture	3.0
Expensing of multiperiod timber growing costs	1.8
Percentage depletion, nonfuel minerals	1.4
Expensing of certain multiperiod agriculture costs	0.9
Expensing of soil and water conservation expenses	0.3
Five-year carryback period for farming net operating losses	0.3
Income averaging for farmers	0.2
Special rules for mining reclamation reserves	0.2
Expensing of exploration costs, nonfuel minerals	0.2
Reforestation tax breaks	0.1
Solvent farmers treated as bankrupt on loans	0.1
Exclusion of cost-sharing payments	0.1
Deferral of gain on sale of farm refiners	0.1
TOTAL	$8.6

Source: Same as Table 1.1.

Expensing multiperiod timber growing costs. Generally, costs must be capitalized when goods are produced for inventory. Timber production, however, was specifically exempted from these multiperiod cost capitalization rules, allowing for immediate deductions.

Credit and seven-year amortization for reforestation. A special 10 percent tax credit is allowed for up to $10,000 invested annually in clearing land and planting trees for the production of timber. Similarly, $10,000 of forestation investment may be amortized over a seven-year period. Without this preference, the amount would have to be capitalized and could be deducted only when the trees were sold or harvested (say, twenty or more years later). Moreover, the forestation investment that is amortizable is not reduced by any of the investment credit that is allowed.

Expensing certain capital outlays. Farmers, except for certain agricultural corporations and partnerships, are allowed to deduct certain investments in feed and fertilizer, as well as for soil and water conservation measures. Expensing is allowed, even though these expenditures are for inventories held beyond the end of the year or for capital improvements that would otherwise be capitalized.

Expensing periodic livestock and crop production costs. Raising livestock and growing crops with a production period of less than two years are exempted from normal cost capitalization rules. Farmers planting orchards, building farm facilities for their own use, or producing goods for sale with longer production periods also may elect not to capitalize certain costs. But if they do, they must apply straight-line depreciation to all depreciable property they use in farming.

Loans forgiven solvent farmers. Farmers are granted another special tax treatment—exemption from taxes on certain forgiven debt. Normally, loan forgiveness is treated as income of the borrower. The borrower must either report the income right away or reduce his or her recoverable basis in the property to which the loan relates (leading to lesser depreciation deductions or a larger taxable gain when the property is sold). In the case of bankrupt debtors, however, loan forgiveness does not result in any income tax liability (currently or in the future). Farmers with forgiven debt are treated as "bankrupt" for tax purposes (even though they are solvent) and thus are never taxed on their forgiven loans.

FINANCIAL INSTITUTIONS (NONINSURANCE)

Before the 1986 Tax Reform Act, it was rare to find a bank (or savings and loan or credit union) that paid any significant amount in federal income taxes. Reforms have lessened the tax breaks for financial institutions (most notably, limits on their ability to deduct interest costs for carrying tax-exempt bonds). But financial institutions still enjoy substantial tax subsidies. In many cases these subsidies are not, however, limited to, nor easily allocable to, the financial industry. Financial institutions, for example, benefit greatly from many of the multinational subsidies. The tax breaks limited to the finance industry are expected to reduce federal revenues by $6.9 billion over the next five years (see Table 2.13). The major industry-specific tax breaks listed in the official tax expenditure budget are:

Bad-debt reserves. Commercial banks with less than $500 million in assets, mutual savings banks, and savings and loan associations are permitted to deduct so-called additions to bad-debt reserves that exceed their actual losses on bad loans. The deduction for additions to loss reserves allowed qualifying mutual savings banks and savings and loan associations is 8 percent of otherwise taxable income. To qualify, the thrift institutions must maintain a specified fraction of their assets in the form of mortgages, primarily residential.

TABLE 2.13
FINANCIAL INSTITUTIONS (NONINSURANCE) 2000–2004
($ BILLIONS)

Exemption of credit union income	6.7
Excess bad-debt reserves of financial institutions	0.2
TOTAL	6.9

Source: Same as Table 1.1.

Credit union income. Unlike the case for banks and thrifts, the earnings of credit unions not distributed to members as interest or dividends are exempt from income tax.

BUSINESS MEALS AND ENTERTAINMENT

It is a fundamental (and usually honored) income tax principle that personal outlays, whether for a family car, a house, food, or entertainment, should *not* be deductible in computing net income.[14] If the income tax laws generally allowed people to deduct their personal expenses, there would be little or nothing left to tax (except savings).[15]

To be sure, when taxpayers assert that some of their apparently personal outlays also have a business purpose, the issues are not always clear-cut. Although the tax code ostensibly allows deductions only for "necessary" business expenses, this rule is liberally interpreted when a business purpose clearly predominates. The law does not limit deductions for office furnishings, for example, to the cheapest available.

But when the personal character of an outlay dominates, the tax code usually does not allow a deduction. Consistent with this principle, current law recognizes that eating and entertainment expenses are personal when someone makes such outlays solely on his or her own behalf. Strangely, however, when a meal or recreational activity is shared with a business associate or a potential client or customer, the tax law generally allows half of the amount spent to be written off.

Specifically, meals that bear a "reasonable and proximate relationship to a trade or business" are 50 percent deductible if they occur under circumstances that are "conducive to a business discussion." There is no requirement that business actually be discussed, either before, during, or after the meal. The fact that such a rule would be unenforceable highlights the difficulties of allowing deductions for essentially personal expenses. Entertainment outlays are 50 percent deductible if the taxpayer has more than a general expectation of deriving income or a specific trade or business benefit (other than goodwill) from the activity or, more liberally, if the entertainment is directly preceded or followed by a substantial and bona fide business discussion (such as a business meal).

Analytically, the proper taxpayer in the case of meals and entertainment benefits should be the person who is fed or entertained. Thus, the theoretically correct treatment of such benefits would be to tax the recipients on the value of the benefits they receive. Denying deductions to payers, however, would produce roughly the same result and would be considerably easier to administer.

The official tax expenditure budgets do not list the meals and entertainment deduction as a tax expenditure. I have nonetheless estimated its cost at $36 billion over the next five years.

DEBT FOR STOCK

Another tax reduction mechanism that is not listed in the official tax expenditure budgets is the use of debt in situations where stock has been the traditional means of raising capital. Allowing deductions of interest payments on debt in such instances, however, in which dividend payments on equity would be taxed, is an evasion of normal tax practice.

The use of "junk bonds" and other types of debt that are more like stocks than real borrowing helped fuel a wave of leveraged buyouts and other debt-for-stock transactions in the 1980s. From 1985 to 1990 more than $1 trillion in new corporate indebtedness was incurred, accompanied by $54 billion in corporate stock retirements—a combination that cost the federal Treasury some $20–30 billion a year in lost corporate taxes.

GOODWILL

Many companies that have acquired other companies have taken extremely aggressive positions on their tax returns in an attempt to write off what they paid for "goodwill" and similar intangible assets (like brand names) that generally do not decline in value over time. Allowing assets to be written off when they have not declined in value has no pure tax policy rationale. Yet this practice is not included in the official tax expenditure lists.

OTHER BUSINESS AND INVESTMENT TAX BREAKS

There are a number of other business and investment tax subsidies (see Table 2.14, page 136). The official tax expenditure budgets incorporate:

TABLE 2.14
OTHER BUSINESS AND INVESTMENT, 2000–2004
($ BILLIONS)

Low-income housing credit	18.2
Special ESOP rules	5.8
Installment sales	3.9
Empowerment zones	2.0
Other	62.6
Graduated corporate income tax rates	27.1
Corporate charitable deductions	18.7
Deferral of interest on savings bonds	5.9
Exclusion from net operating loss limits for bankrupt corporations.	2.5
Completed contract rules	1.1
Permanent exceptions from imputed interest rules	1.0
Cancellation of indebtedness	0.1
Cash accounting other than agriculture	0.6
Credit for disabled access expenditures	0.4
Investment credit for fixing up structures	0.1
Exemption of certain mutuals' and co-ops' income	0.3
Work opportunity tax credit	1.5
Welfare-to-work tax credit	0.3
Expensing of magazine circulation expenditures	0.2
Special rules for magazine, book, and record returns	0.1
Exclusion of contribution to construction of water and sewer facilities.	0.1
Tax credit for employer-paid FICA taxes on tips	1.8
Expensing redevelopment costs in contaminated areas	0.3
Tax credit for orphan drug research	0.5
TOTAL	92.5

Source: Same as Table 1.1.

Low-income housing credit. A tax credit for investment in new, substantially rehabilitated, and certain unrehabilitated low-income housing is allowed, worth 70 percent of construction or rehabilitation costs (and taken over ten years with interest). For federally subsidized projects and those involving unrehabilitated low-income housing, the credit is worth 30 percent of costs. In addition, investors are allowed to take depreciation write-offs as if they had not received this large tax credit subsidy.

Employee Stock Ownership Plan (ESOP) provisions. A special type of employee benefit plan, ESOPs are tax-exempt. Corporate contributions of stock to the ESOP *are* deductible by the company as part of employee compensation. But they are not included in the employees' gross income for tax purposes until they are paid out as benefits. There are other tax breaks for ESOPs: (1) annual employer contributions are subject to less restrictive limits (percentages of employees' cash compensation) than regular pension plans; (2) ESOPs may borrow to purchase employer stock under an agreement with the employer that the debt will be serviced by the corporation's (tax-deductible) payment of a portion of wages (excludable by the employees) to service the loan; (3) lenders to ESOPs may exclude half the interest they receive from their gross income; (4) employees who sell appreciated company stock to the ESOP may defer any taxes due until they withdraw benefits; and (5) dividends paid on ESOP-held stock are deductible by the corporate employer. In theory, tax subsidies for ESOPs are intended to increase ownership of corporations by their employees.

Real property installment sales. When a business sells a product, normal accounting (and tax rules) include the proceeds in gross income. That is true even if the seller lends the buyer the money to buy the product and the buyer pays in installments (typically with interest).[14] But business sellers of real estate can put off paying tax on installment sales of up to $5 million in outstanding obligations.

Empowerment zones. Businesses in designated "economically depressed areas" will get $2 billion in special tax breaks over the next five years, including an employer wage credit, increased depreciation write-offs, and tax-exempt financing. There is also a tax credit for gifts to certain community development corporations and special tax breaks for the District of Columbia.

Reduced corporate income tax rates for smaller corporations. Smaller corporations are taxed at lower rates than the 35 percent regular corporate rate, with the tax savings from the lower rates phased out for larger companies (see Table 2.15, page 138). As a result, statutory corporate

TABLE 2.15
CORPORATE TAX RATES

Taxable Income ($)	Rate (%)
0	15
50,000	25
75,000	34
100,000	39
335,000	34
10,000,000	35
15,000,000	38

Source: Author calculations.

rates bounce around a lot. The rationale for this tax expenditure is that it helps small business. Why small businesses should be favored over large ones is unclear. In addition, the lower rates can be used by individual corporate owners to avoid higher personal income tax rates.

Exceptions to imputed interest rules. The tax laws generally try to treat interest paid or received based on the substance of a transaction, not on how lenders and borrowers might try to characterize the interest payments to minimize their tax liability. Suppose, for instance, that someone borrows $10 million and promises to pay back $15 million in a lump sum four years later. The tax code would treat the interest on this loan just as if the interest payments were made annually. Thus, the lender would have to include $1.25 million of interest in income each year (roughly speaking), and the borrower could deduct a corresponding amount.

Likewise, if a borrower promises to pay $1 million plus interest at 10 percent on a one-year loan—for a total repayment of $1.1 million—but only gets $900,000 from the lender, the tax law would treat this as what it actually is—a $900,000 loan at 22.2 percent interest. (This could matter a lot if the lender is in a high tax bracket and the borrower in a low one.) The tax code generally requires at least a market rate of interest.

There are exceptions to these general rules for accounting for interest expense or income, however. First of all, there is a $250,000 general exception. Second, sellers of farms and small businesses worth less than $1 million, with a note taken back from the purchaser, are exempt. And, third, "points" on mortgage loans used to purchase a home are treated as prepaid interest deductible in the year paid rather than requiring that the interest deductions be spread out over the life of the loan.

U.S. savings bonds. Unlike, say, interest from corporate bonds, regular Treasury bonds, or savings accounts, interest on U.S. savings bonds is not taxed until the savings bonds are redeemed. This tax deferral is like an interest-free loan from the government. The 2000–2004 cost is $5.9 billion.

PENSIONS, IRAS, ETC.

Normally, people do not get a tax deduction for the money they save (if they did, this country would have a consumption tax, not an income tax; see Table 2.16). But employer contributions to pension plans and certain other kinds of personal retirement savings are excluded from individuals' adjusted gross incomes (see Box 1, page 140). Likewise, investment income earned by pension funds and other qualifying retirement plans is not taxed when earned. Instead, people pay tax on their retirement savings and accrued investment income only when they withdraw the funds after retirement.

Tax breaks for employer retirement contributions were first established as an incentive for corporations to provide pensions to their

TABLE 2.16
RETIREMENT AND SAVINGS, 2000–2004
($ BILLIONS)

Pensions, Keoghs, IRAs	558.5
Employer pension plans	452.5
Individual Retirement Accounts	77.3
Keogh self-employed plans	28.7
Other Savings	1.3
Education IRAs and state tuition plan deferrals	1.2
Medical Savings Accounts	0.1

Source: Same as Table 1.1.

Box 1
Limits on Tax Deferrals for Retirement Savings

Employer pensions: In general, tax deferrals for employer pension plans are limited to $30,000 in employer contributions per worker per year. Alternatively, in the case of defined benefit plans, the maximum annual pension payment per work cannot exceed about $120,000 (indexed for inflation).

Self-employed pension plans: Self-employed persons can make deductible contributions to their own retirement (Keogh) plans equal to 25 percent of their income, up to a maximum of $30,000 per year.

401(k) plans and tax-sheltered annuities: Limited amounts ($10,500 in 2001, being phased up to $15,000 in 2005) can be excluded from an employee's adjusted gross income under a qualified cash or deferred arrangement with the employer, known as a 401(k) plan. A worker's own contribution of a similar amount may be excluded annually from the worker's adjusted gross income when placed in a tax-sheltered annuity.

Deductible Individual Retirement Accounts (IRAs): Workers can deduct annual contributions to an IRA of $2,000 per year (or total compensation, if less). For couples, the maximum deduction is $4,000. These amounts are being phased up and will be $5,000 for single individuals and $10,000 for couples in 2008. All taxpayers without employer-provided retirement plans are eligible for IRA deductions.

In addition, even taxpayers whose employers do provide retirement benefits can take IRA deductions if their incomes are below certain levels. For couples with employer plans, IRA deductions are phased out between $50,000 and $60,000 of adjusted gross income. For single people with employer plans, the phaseout is between $30,000 and $40,000. The income level of the phaseout range is being increased annually. In 2007 it will be $80,000 to $100,000 for married couples and $50,000 to $60,000 for singles. Beyond these income limits, taxpayers with employer plans can still make nondeductible contributions to IRAs and defer tax on investment income until retirement.

Backloaded ("Roth") IRAs: A nondeductible IRA contribution can be made to a Roth IRA. Income to the Roth IRA is not taxed, and withdrawals are tax-free if the IRA has been opened for at least five years and the taxpayer

BOX 1 (CONTINUED)
LIMITS ON TAX DEFERRALS FOR RETIREMENT SAVINGS

either is (a) at least fifty-nine and a half years old, (b) dies, (c) is disabled, or (d) purchases a first time home. The maximum contribution is phased out between $150,000 and $160,000 for couples ($95,000 and $110,000 for single filers) of adjusted gross income. Total IRA contributions, Roth and ordinary, cannot exceed $2,000 ($4,000 for joint filers.)

workers. To further the goal of ensuring that pension benefits are not limited to business owners, managers and highly paid employees, "antidiscrimination" rules have been gradually strengthened over time.

In general, under current law, pension contributions or benefits must be based on an equal percentage of salary for all eligible workers (up to the maximum contribution of $30,000 a year). Full-time workers must gain a full right to accrued pension benefits (that is, benefits must "vest") after five years on the job, or, alternatively, benefits can vest at 20 percent a year from the third to the seventh year of work.

As with other exclusions of income, pension tax breaks are upside-down subsidies that benefit those in higher tax brackets more than those in lower tax brackets. Although pension tax deferrals clearly favor the well-off in terms of their direct benefits, they have probably helped enhance retirement savings for ordinary workers. In fact, the distribution of pension *payouts* to retired people is far more equitable than the distribution of income overall. For example, families with incomes below $50,000 have 31 percent of total income from all sources, but get 43 percent of total pension income. In contrast, people making more than $200,000 get 23 percent of the nation's total income but only 6 percent of total pensions (see Table 2.17, page 142).

Treatment similar to that given corporate pensions was extended to unincorporated businesses and later to Individual Retirement Accounts for people without employer-provided pensions. In 1981, eligibility for tax-deductible IRAs was granted even to workers with pensions, but that expanded IRA tax break was scaled back in 1986. In 1997 so-called Roth IRAs became available for more workers with pensions.

TABLE 2.17
DISTRIBUTION OF TAXABLE PENSIONS

| Income Group | All Families | | % of Pension Income |
	% of Families	% of All Income	
$0–10,000	12.3	1.6	1.2
$10–20,000	19.9	5.8	5.9
$20–30,000	16.4	8.0	11.3
$30–40,000	11.7	7.9	13.3
$40–50,000	9.2	8.1	11.6
$50–75,000	14.7	17.7	23.0
$75–100,000	6.8	11.5	13.9
$100–200,000	6.2	16.1	14.2
$200,000+	2.1	23.4	5.7

Source: Microsimulation Tax Model, Institute on Taxation and Economic Policy, Washington, D.C., March 2000.

Retirement-directed tax breaks, particularly IRAs, have some-times been touted as "savings incentives." Yet, despite a major ex-pansion in the use of these tax subsidies over time, national savings have not improved. Indeed, the abject failure of IRAs to augment savings (along with their skyrocketing cost) was one reason IRAs were scaled back in the 1986 Tax Reform Act.[17]

OTHER SAVINGS

New forms of tax-favored savings arrived in 1997. These took shape as Medical Savings Accounts, a tax break for guaranteed state tuition savings programs, and the bizarrely named "Educational Individual Retirement Accounts." The latter operate like Roth IRAs but have nothing to do with retirement. Instead, they allow a contribution of $500 per year per child to save for future educational costs. The revenue loss for Medical Savings Accounts is trivial, but they offer an opportunity for better-off, healthy taxpayers to self-insure against noncatastrophic health care costs. If MSAs ever amount to much they could cause health insurance premiums to rise for those remaining in the insurance pools.

3

PERSONAL TAX EXPENDITURES

ITEMIZED DEDUCTIONS

While some itemized deductions lack a strong tax policy basis and can be criticized as inefficient or unfair subsidies, others can be seriously defended on tax policy grounds. One common characteristic of itemized deductions is that they are all upside-down subsidies. Wealthier taxpayers also are much more likely to have itemized deductions in excess of the standard deduction, making the option of itemizing more valuable to the better-off (see Table 3.1, page 144).

The total expected cost of itemized deductions, for the 2000–2004 period is $613 billion (see Table 3.2, page 145). Note that this amount is less than the sum of the tax expenditure amount of each itemized deduction. This is because of the interaction with the standard deduction. For example, assume a couple has only two itemized deductions: $8,000 in state personal income tax and $3,000 in charitable deductions. If this couple were not itemizing, their standard deduction would be $7,200. If the charitable deduction were abolished, the couple would lose $3,000 in deductions. If the state personal income tax deduction were repealed, they would lose $3,800 in deductions because their deductions cannot go below the standard deduction. The total loss in deductions for this couple if the charitable and the state personal income tax deductions were both repealed is not the sum of the two components but only the $3,800 that would take them down to the standard deduction.

TABLE 3.1 1999 TAX SAVINGS FROM ITEMIZED DEDUCTIONS

Income Group $-000	% of All Units	All Deductions		State and Local Taxes		Mortgage Interest		Charitable Gifts		Medical Costs	
		% With	Average Benefit*	% With	Average Benefit*	% With	Average Benefit*	% With	Average Benefit*	% With	Average Benefit*
$0–10	12.3	0.3	1	0.1	0	0.2	0	0.2	0	0.1	0
$10–20	19.9	2.5	10	2.1	2	1.8	8	1.7	2	1.1	4
$20–30	16.4	8.9	49	8.3	20	7.1	35	6.6	10	3.0	12
$30–40	11.7	19.5	142	19.3	66	16.3	97	16.8	38	6.1	31
$40–50	9.2	32.6	317	32.3	168	28.2	237	29.0	72	7.6	39
$50–75	14.7	56.9	777	56.4	434	50.6	588	52.8	186	6.3	40
$75–100	6.8	77.4	1,852	76.6	1,055	70.3	1,308	73.9	415	5.4	64
$100–200	6.2	88.8	4,004	88.0	2,085	78.2	2,362	86.2	794	4.1	75
$200	2.1	90.8	15,597	89.2	8,908	75.1	5,260	90.2	4,099	1.7	115
ALL	100.0	28.3	875	27.9	480	24.7	473	26.1	205	3.7	27

Note: "All deductions" includes deductions not shown separately here. Details do not sum to total because of standard deduction offset, itemized deduction disallowance at high-income levels and Alternative Minimum Tax Effects. "Units" = Families + Individuals not families.
*Averages for all families and individuals in each group
Source: Microsimulation Tax Model, Institute on taxation and Economic Policy, Washington, D.C., March 2000.

TABLE 3.2
ITEMIZED DEDUCTIONS, 2000–2004 ($ BILLIONS)

Mortgage interest	309.7
State and local taxes (except home property)	207.8
Property taxes (homes)	110.7
Charitable contributions	146.0
Medical expenses	23.8
Casualty losses	1.4
Standard deduction offset	−186.9
TOTAL	612.5

Source: Same as Table 1.1.

Mortgage interest on owner-occupied homes. Homeowners who itemize deductions can deduct mortgage interest on their primary and secondary residences. This tax expenditure is projected at $310 billion from 2000 through 2004. The regular mortgage interest deduction is limited to interest on debt no greater than the homeowner's basis in the residence, and the loan is limited as well to no more than $1 million (for debt incurred after October 13, 1987). Interest on home-equity loans on debt of up to $100,000 also is deductible, irrespective of the purpose of borrowing (provided that the debt does not exceed the fair market value of the residence). The home-equity interest deduction is an exception to the general denial of deductions for personal interest.

Like all subsidies structured as personal tax deductions, these interest write-offs lead to upside-down effects: the higher a person's income (and tax bracket), the greater the subsidy. This leads to consequences that would probably not be found politically acceptable in a direct spending subsidy for home purchases.

- If a family making $45,000 borrows $75,000 to buy a home, the federal government will offset about 13 percent of its total mortgage payments, a subsidy worth about $81 per month. But if a family making $500,000 takes out a $360,000 mortgage to buy a house, the government will subsidize about 35 percent of its mortgage payments, worth $1,020 a month.[1] On average, mortgage interest deductions are worth $5,260 a year each to taxpayers making more than $200,000 but only $336 a year to families earning between $30,000 and $75,000.

There is no subsidy for those who lack itemized deductions in excess of the standard deduction. These are usually lower-income taxpayers who do not have significant state personal income tax and other deductions. In 2001, about 33 million tax returns were expected to show a deduction for mortgage interest. That compares to about 70 million homeowning families. Thus, more than half of all homeowners get no tax reduction at all from the mortgage interest deduction. Of those, some, of course, have no mortgages. But homeowners who do not have high enough mortgage interest payments (although they may still have substantial mortgage payments overall), plus taxpayers who rent rather than own, make for a very large group that gets no help from the mortgage interest subsidy.[2]

It seems obvious that a $60 billion-a-year direct government housing subsidy program with such bizarre effects would have no chance at all of being enacted. Nevertheless, the mortgage deduction has been on the books so long and is relied on by so many people that curtailing it would have to be done slowly and gradually to avoid serious unfairness during the transition. Some reformers have suggested eliminating the home-equity loan loophole and the deduction for second homes and also lowering the cap on regular mortgage loans eligible for the deduction from the current $1 million.

State and local taxes. Itemizers can deduct the personal income and property taxes they pay to their state and local governments. (Sales taxes used to be deductible but no longer are, in part because it was very difficult for people to keep track of what they actually paid in sales taxes and because the alternative sales tax deduction tables provided by the IRS were not very accurate.) The projected cost to the government for this tax expenditure over the next five years is $319 billion. Of this, $111 billion is for home property taxes. The rationale for the tax deduction for state and local taxes is that people should not be taxed on income that does not directly benefit them personally but that they are required to hand over in taxes to serve the general good.

Charitable contributions. Contributions to charitable, religious, and certain other nonprofit organizations are allowed as itemized deductions for individuals, generally up to 50 percent of adjusted gross income. Taxpayers who donate assets to charitable or educational organizations can deduct the assets' full value without any tax on appreciation. Corporations also can deduct charitable contributions, up to 10 percent of their pretax income. Individuals will have their taxes reduced by $146 billion over the next five years by this tax expenditure. Corporate income taxes will be reduced by $19 billion.

The basic principle behind the tax deduction for charitable donations is a defensible one: people should not be taxed on income that does not benefit them personally but that they instead give away for the public good. (This is the same as the rationale for the deduction for state and local taxes.) In other words, if someone earns $1,000 and gives it away to charity, it is reasonable not to tax that person on that $1,000 in earnings. The normal way it works in the case of cash gifts is that the donor includes the $1,000 in gross income and deducts the $1,000 gift in computing taxable income. Net result: no tax on the income given to charity.

But there are abuses. Take someone who has $1,000 worth of stock originally bought for $100. If that person sells the stock and gives the $1,000 to charity, the $900 gain will be included in gross income, and a deduction will be taken for the donation. The net tax on the income given to charity will be zero. Fair enough.

Suppose, however, that instead our taxpayer gives the stock itself directly to charity. That should not produce a different bottom-line tax result. After all, there is no real distinction. But under the regular income tax rules there is a huge difference. Not only will the taxpayer get a deduction for the $100 in earnings originally used to buy the stock, but there will also be a deduction for the $900 in appreciation that is not included in adjusted gross income. As a result, this person will avoid paying taxes on $900 of other income not given to charity. This strange result is the equivalent of allowing someone who sells the stock and makes a cash gift to take a double deduction for the stock's increased value.

Although often criticized, the loophole for donations of appreciated property was a fixture in the tax code for many years. In 1986, however, the Tax Reform Act limited these excessive charitable deductions in connection with the alternative minimum tax—which is supposed to ensure that all high-income people pay at least some significant federal income tax no matter how many tax preferences they may utilize under the regular tax code. After 1986, in computing taxable income under the minimum tax, taxpayers who made charitable donations of appreciated property no longer got better treatment than cash donors. In 1993 the tax break was restored by repealing the 1986 reform. Another problem with allowing the charitable deduction on appreciation is the difficulty in the valuation of donations of art and other collectibles.

Medical expenses. Personal, out-of-pocket outlays for medical care (including the costs of prescription drugs) exceeding 7.5 percent of adjusted gross income are deductible. This tax expenditure will reduce taxpayer liability by $24 billion over the next five years. The rationale for the deduction is that extraordinary out-of-pocket medical expenses reduce a family's ability to pay taxes.

Because of the floor, only about one in twenty-three taxpayers utilizes this deduction in any given year. A family with income of $50,000, for example, can deduct only medical expenses above $3,750. Because of the floor (and because a third of the families who do take the medical deduction would otherwise use the standard deduction), the average subsidy rate is quite low, only about 8 percent of the extraordinary medical expenses claimed. About half of the total tax savings go to families making between $30,000 and $75,000. In this group, one out of fifteen taxpayers claims the deduction. Their average medical expenses are about $8,000, with about $5,000 of that deductible. Their average tax saving from the deduction is $560.

Casualty losses. People who buy property and casualty insurance ordinarily cannot deduct its cost. Unlucky families or those who planned poorly who suffer a large uninsured loss owing to casualty or theft can sometimes deduct such a loss—but only if their total losses during a year are more than 10 percent of their adjusted gross income (and if they itemize deductions). Because of the floor, very few taxpayers take the casualty loss deduction (only 99,459 did so in 1999). The number taking the deduction and its cost to the Treasury seems to fluctuate depending on the level of natural disasters in a year. The projected cost over the next five years is $1.4 billion.

Although the casualty loss deduction could have some appeal on ability-to-pay grounds (similar to the deduction for extraordinary medical expenses), one can reasonably ask whether what amounts to a government backup to the private property insurance system makes much sense.

FRINGE BENEFITS

Tax subsidies are available for a wide range of employee compensation that is paid not in cash but in fringe benefits (see Table 3.3). Tax policy analysts have long complained about the disparity between cash wages and benefits. Many wonder, for example, why a person who pays cash for insurance should be taxed more heavily than another person who gets insurance as a fringe benefit (and accepts lower cash wages). Others point out that tax subsidies for certain kinds of spending may encourage it at the expense of otherwise more satisfying outlays. Yet, despite these fairness and economic issues, there rarely is any political interest in changing the tax treatment of fringe benefits, in large part because the benefits are so broadly dispersed among the public.

TABLE 3.3
FRINGE BENEFITS, 2000–2004
($ BILLIONS)

Employer-paid health insurance	380.3
Other fringe benefit exclusions	86.7
Miscellaneous fringe benefits	36.7
Group term life insurance	10.1
Employer-paid transportation benefits	14.7
Cafeteria plan fringe benefits (nonhealth)	9.9
Employer-provided child care	3.0
Employee meals and lodging (nonmilitary)	4.0
Parsonage allowances	2.0
Voluntary employee benefits association benefits	4.0
Accident and disability insurance	1.0
Employee awards	0.7
Employer education assistance	0.7
TOTAL	467.0

Source: Same as Table 1.1.

Employer-paid medical insurance and expenses. Employee compensation in the form of payments for health insurance premiums and other medical expenses is deducted as a business expense by employers but is not included in employees' gross income. The cost of this tax expenditure through 2004 is projected to be $380 billion.

The exclusion for health insurance benefits does not have much of the upside-down subsidy character that is typical of tax deductions. The tax break reduces both income and Social Security payroll taxes, and marginal tax rates on wages, including Social Security taxes, run at about 30 percent for the vast majority of working families (although the best-off 1 percent of taxpayers are in a 40 percent-plus bracket). Moreover, because health insurance premiums are basically a flat amount per family, regardless of earnings level, the size of the health insurance tax subsidy actually declines as a share of income as income rises.

An additional advantage of employer-provided health insurance over a system where employees would individually seek health insurance on their own is the societal benefit of risk pooling. The health insurance tax subsidy does not, however, benefit the uninsured, who tend to be lower-income workers.

Tax breaks for nonhealth fringe benefits. These provisions (excluding pensions, discussed earlier) are estimated to cost about $87 billion over the next five years. They are:

- *Other employer-provided insurance benefits.* Many employers cover part or all the cost of premiums or payments for: (a) employees' life insurance benefits; (b) accident and disability benefits; (c) death benefits; and (d) supplementary unemployment benefits. The amounts are deductible by the employers and are excluded as well from employees' gross incomes for tax purposes. Somewhat like health insurance subsidies, the percentage distribution of these other fringe benefit tax breaks among the working populace is relatively evenhanded as tax subsidies go (although higher-income employees are probably much more likely to get them).

- *Exclusion of employee parking expenses and employer-provided transit passes.* Employee parking expenses paid for by employers are excluded from the employees' income, up to $175 a month, indexed for inflation. (Parking at facilities owned by the employer is not counted as a tax break.) Some environmentalists charged that this tax subsidy encourages driving at the expense of mass transit. So Congress extended the subsidy to employer-paid transit passes, tokens, and fare cards (so long as the total value of the benefit does not exceed $65 per month, indexed for inflation).

- *Cafeteria plans.* Cafeteria plans allow employees to choose from a selection of fringe benefits, including some that are not subject to tax. Those fringe benefits that would be excludable on their own are nontaxable. Cafeteria plans are more likely to benefit to better-off employees in higher marginal tax brackets, as they are more likely to choose fringe benefits that receive the tax preference.

- *Other fringe benefits.* Several other employee benefits are not counted in employees' income, although the employers' costs for these benefits are deductible business expenses. Such exclusions cover, among other things, child care, meals and lodging, ministers' housing allowances, and the rental value of parsonages.

EARNED INCOME TAX CREDIT

The earned income tax credit (EITC) is designed to supplement the wages of low- and moderate-income workers, primarily working families with children (see Table 3.4, page 152). It is available whether or not a family owes income taxes. That is, eligible workers can get a "tax refund" even if the credit exceeds what they otherwise owe in taxes. Over the next five years the credit will reduce tax payments by $23 billion. An additional $135 billion will be refunded.

As a result of changes adopted in 1993, in 1999 the EITC is equal to 40 percent of the first $9,550 in wages for families with two or more children—for a maximum of $3,820. It is 34 percent of the first $6,800 in wages for a family with one child (maximum $2,312). The credit is phased out between $12,460 and $30.600 in income for two-child-plus families and between $12,460 and $26,930 for one-child families. Low-income childless workers (ages twenty-five to sixty-four) can get a small credit equal to 7.65 percent of up to $4,510 in wages ($347), phased out between $5,670 and $10,200. All these amounts are indexed for inflation.

TABLE 3.4
THE EARNED INCOME TAX CREDIT IN 1999

Income Group	% of Total Benefits	Average Benefit	
		Families with	All Families
$0–10,000	18.9%	$1,042	$347
$10–20,000	53.3%	$2,223	$606
$20–30,000	24.6%	$1,338	$339
$30–40,000	3.3%	$979	$63
$40,000+	—	—	—
ALL FAMILIES	100.0%	$1,568	$226

Source: Microsimulation Tax Model, Institute on Taxation and Economic Policy, Washington, D.C., March 2000.

OTHER PERSONAL TAX EXPENDITURES

Tax-free Social Security benefits for retired workers. Social Security benefits are essentially supplemented for most recipients by the fact that, unlike private pensions, they are largely not subject to income tax (see Tables 3.5, page 153, and 3.6, page 154). This tax break— estimated to cost $136 billion over the next five years—is phased out, however, for better-off retirees. Retired couples, for example, begin paying taxes on part of their Social Security benefits when their total income exceeds about $40,000. The portion subject to tax rises gradually and eventually reaches 85 percent (at about $70,000 in total retirement income for couples). Thus, the tax code enhances the already progressive nature of Social Security benefits received compared to taxes paid into the fund during people's working years. (Similar rules apply to railroad retirement benefits.)

Child credit. The child credit was adopted in the 1997 tax act. It is $500 for each child under age seventeen (see Table 3.7, page 155). The credit is phased out at a rate of $50 per $1,000 of modified adjusted gross income above $110,000 ($75,000 for singles). The child credit may be partially refundable for taxpayers with three or more children (usually limited to the amount by which a

TABLE 3.5
OTHER PERSONAL, 2000–2004 ($ BILLIONS)

Social Security benefits (exclusion)	135.6
Child Credit	92.4
Capital gains on homes	81.8
Workmen's compensation, etc.	56.6
Education credits and deductions	42.4
Soldiers and veterans exclusions	26.0
Child and dependent care credit	11.3
Elderly and blind	10.4
Other personal	22.0
Exclusion of scholarships & fellowships	6.1
Parental personal, exemption for students age 19+	4.6
Deduction for self-employment health insurance	9.2
Exclusion of certain foster care payments	1.5
Exclusion of savings bond interest for education	0.1
Adoption credit and exclusion	0.7
TOTAL	478.6

Source: Same as Table 1.1.

taxpayer's FICA tax exceeds refundable EITC). The child credit is projected to reduce federal personal income tax collections by $92 billion from 2000 through 2004.

Capital gains on home sales. A home seller can exclude from tax up to $500,000 ($250,000 for singles), of the capital gains from the sale of a principal residence. The exclusion may not be used more than once every two years. Cost is $82 billion from 2000 through 2004.

Workmen's compensation, public assistance, and disabled coal miner benefits. Workmen's compensation payments to disabled workers, welfare payments, and disability payments to former coal miners out of the black lung trust fund are not subject to the income tax, although they clearly are income to their recipients. The cost of these "tax expenditures" is not insignificant—$60 billion from 2000 to 2004—mostly

TABLE 3.6
TAX SAVINGS FROM EXCLUSION
OF SOCIAL SECURITY BENEFITS

Income Group	% of Savings	Average Savings ($)*
$0–10	0.1	5
$10–20	11.8	354
$20–30	28.4	1,143
$30–40	27.7	1,540
$40–50	18.7	1,549
$50–75	11.9	723
$75–100	1.3	188
$100–200	0.1	15
$200+	0.0	4
ALL	100.0	728

*Average for taxpayers with Social Security. Comparison is to requiring all recipients to include 85 percent of their benefits in adjusted gross income.
Source: Microsimulation Tax Model, Institute on Taxation and Economic Policy, Washington, D.C., March 2000.

reflecting the exclusion of workmen's compensation. Most of the beneficiaries of these tax subsidies, especially those getting welfare payments, are low-income people.

Education credits and deductions. The HOPE tax credit, Lifetime Learning tax credit, and the deduction for student loan interest are tax preferences for postsecondary education, with the two credits targeted to low- and moderate-income families. Concerns have been raised that the real benefit of the credits goes to colleges and universities through reduced financial aid payments and higher tuition instead of to students and their families.

Benefits and allowances to soldiers and veterans. Housing and meals provided military personnel, either in cash or in kind, are excluded from income subject to tax. Most military pension income received by current disabled retired veterans is excluded from their income subject to tax. All compensation attribute to death or disability and pensions paid by the Veterans Administration are excluded from

TABLE 3.7
$500 PER CHILD TAX CREDITS IN 1999

Income Group	Number of Families with Children (thousands)	Number with Any per Child Credit (thousands)	Average per Dependent Child ($)
$0–10	3,723	19	1.00
$10–20	6,833	2,231	67.67
$20–30	6,054	4,201	257.16
$30–40	4,929	4,061	387.16
$40–50	4,500	3,891	414.95
$50–75	8,723	7,557	417.47
$75–100	4,256	3,516	394.90
$100–200	3,874	1,657	180.89
$200+	1,407	—	—
TOTALS	44,467	27,143	$ 269.00

Note: Average credits are lower than the nominal $500 per child amount because: (a) the credit is limited to dependent children under age 17; (b) the credit is generally limited to income taxes before credits; and (c) the credit is phased out at high income levels.
Source: Microsimulation Tax Model, Institute on Taxation and Economic Policy, Washington D.C., March 2000.

taxable income. In effect, this tax break is in lieu of granting soldiers higher pay while they are in the service. Of course, the benefits of this $26 billion tax subsidy (2000–2004) are considerably higher for those with the highest postmilitary earnings because they depend on a person's tax bracket.

Child and dependent care expenses. Working families with children get a tax credit for a percentage of their child care expenses (see Table 3.8, page 156). Married couples can claim the credit if one spouse works full time and the other works at least part time or goes to school. Single working parents (including divorced or separated parents who have custody of children) also can claim the credit. Child care costs (and loosely related maid service expenses) of up to a maximum $2,400 for one dependent and $4,800 for two or more dependents are eligible for the credit. Unlike the upside-down subsidies provided by most special tax deductions and exclusions, the child care credit's

TABLE 3.8
CHILD CARE CREDITS IN 1999

| Income Group | % with Credit | Average Tax Saving ($) | |
		Families with Credit	All Families
$0–10	—	—	—
$10–20	1.1	$355	4
$20–30	4.2	$423	18
$30–40	6.0	$400	24
$40–50	7.1	$387	28
$50–75	8.6	$402	34
$75–100	9.7	$412	40
$100–200	8.2	$461	38
$200+	4.7	$485	23
TOTALS	4.8	$410	$20

Source: Microsimulation Tax Model, Institute on Taxation and Economic Policy, Washington, D.C., March 2000.

percentage subsidy declines as income rises. Specifically, the credit is equal to 30 percent of qualified child care costs for parents with family incomes of $10,000 or less, phased down to 20 percent at $28,000 or more in income. The 2000–2004 cost of the child care credit is $11.3 billion.

Other tax help for the elderly and the blind. Taxpayers sixty-five or older and blind people get a larger standard deduction (nine out of ten elderly or blind do not itemize). The additional deduction was $1,050 for eligible singles and $850 per spouse for couples (that is, $1,700 if both qualify) in 1999. These amounts are indexed for inflation.

In addition, a very limited number of individuals who are sixty-five or older, or who are permanently disabled, can take a tax credit equal to 15 percent of the sum of their earned and retirement income. Qualified income is limited to no more than $2,500 for single people and for married couples filing a joint return where only one spouse is sixty-five and can be up to $3,750 for joint returns where both spouses are sixty-five or older. These limits are reduced by one-half of the taxpayer's adjusted gross income in excess of $7,500 for single individuals and $10,000 for married couples filing a joint return. The cost of this credit is very small.

The 2000–2004 total cost of these tax breaks for the elderly and disabled are $10 billion.

Scholarship and fellowship income. Scholarships and fellowships granted to students working for an academic degree are not taxable except to the extent they exceed tuition and course-related expenses. The distinction essentially regards scholarships as nontaxable discounts on educational fees but treats any excess amounts as taxable because they constitute payments for services (often the case with fellowships) or coverage of normal living expenses (such as room and board).

Deduction for part of the cost of self-employed health insurance. Self-employed people can deduct 30 percent of their health insurance costs—a scaled-back version of the 100 percent exclusion workers enjoy for employer-provided health insurance. Currently pending legislation would increase the percentage that can be deducted.

U.S. savings bonds for education. The general rule for interest on U.S. savings bonds is that tax is due when the bonds mature. But if savings bonds (and the interest thereon) are used to fund educational expenses, then the deferred tax on the interest is completely forgiven. (The exclusion applies only to bonds issued after 1989.) This exclusion is phased out between $65,250 and $96,900 of adjusted gross income for joint returns and between $43,450 and $59,300 for single and head-of-household returns (at 1996 levels, indexed for inflation). Generally, the income phaseouts effectively limit the tax subsidy to about 15 percent of savings bond interest used to pay for educational expenses.

Dependent students age nineteen or older. Taxpayers can claim personal exemptions for dependent children age nineteen or over who receive parental support payments of $1,000 or more per year, are full-time students, and do not claim a personal exemption on their own tax returns—even if the students would normally not qualify as dependents because the parents do not provide more than half their support. In effect, this allows students to transfer their personal exemptions to their parents—an arrangement beneficial to families in which the parents' marginal tax rate is higher than the student's marginal rate.

Foster care payments. Foster parents provide a home and care for children who are wards of a state, under a contract with the state. Foster parents are not taxed on the payments they receive for their services and their expenses are consequently nondeductible. Though this activity is tax-exempt, it is not likely that much tax would be due if foster parenting were treated as a business, since expenses would be approximately equal to income.

4

CONCLUSION

Tax expenditures represent a significant portion of government spending. They involve programs that range from those highly targeted to special interests to those whose benefits are broadly shared. Half of all tax expenditures go to subsidize business, investment, and savings. Of the rest, most goes to tax expenditures that give a disproportionate share to the well-off. These characteristics would make many such subsidies untenable to the public were they presented in the form of direct spending programs. Some of the government programs carried out through provisions labeled as "tax expenditures" arguably have legitimate tax, social, or economic policy purposes. But while the positive incentive effects of tax breaks are evident only rarely, the distributive effects are far more clear: households and businesses are treated unequally, and the well-off are the ones who, in almost every case, benefit the most.

APPENDIX 1
PERCENTAGE OF BENEFIT OF SELECTED PERSONAL TAX BREAKS GOING TO EACH INCOME GROUP VERSUS PERCENTAGE OF FAMILIES AND INDIVIDUALS IN THOSE GROUPS IN 1999

Income Group (thousands)	% of All Units	Total for Tax Breaks	Low Rates on Capital Gains	Tax-Exempt Bonds	Itemized Deductions	Earned Income Tax Credit	Social Security Exclusion	Dependant Care Credit	Child Credit
$0–10	12	2	0	0	0	19	0	—	0
$10–20	20	8	0	1	0	53	12	4	4
$20–30	16	7	0	2	1	24	28	15	13
$30–40	12	5	0	2	2	3	28	14	16
$40–50	9	5	0	2	3	—	19	13	16
$50–75	15	10	2	6	13	—	12	26	32
$75–100	7	9	3	6	14	—	1	14	14
$100–200	6	16	7	17	28	—	0	12	6
$200+	2	39	87	64	38	—	0	2	0
2000–2004 cost (billions)			$207.2	$57.9	$612.5	$157.7	$135.6	$11.3	$92.4

Note: Units = Families + Individuals not in families.

Source: Microsimulation Tax Model, Institute on Taxation and Economic Policy, Washington, D.C., March 2000.

Appendix 2
Tax Expenditures, Fiscal 2000–2004, Detailed List
($ billions)

	Corporations and Individuals Combined					
	2000	2001	2002	2003	2004	2000–2004
TOTAL ALL TAX EXPENDITURES	**630.7**	**660.5**	**686.6**	**710.5**	**739.0**	**3,427.4**
Tax Expenditures for Business, Investment, and Savings (Corporations & Individuals)						
TOTAL, BUSINESS, INVESTMENT, AND SAVINGS	**315.8**	**332.4**	**344.5**	**352.7**	**366.3**	**1,711.7**
ACCELERATED DEPRECIATION	**39.0**	**40.9**	**40.8**	**40.6**	**41.0**	**202.4**
Accelerated depreciation of machinery & equipment	29.7	31.9	31.6	31.7	32.4	157.4
Accelerated depreciation on rental housing	5.4	5.4	5.4	5.5	5.6	27.2
Accelerated depreciation of buildings except rental housing	2.2	1.7	1.7	1.5	1.2	8.3
Expensing of certain small-equipment investments	1.1	1.4	1.4	1.2	1.1	6.2
Amortization of business start-up costs	0.3	0.3	0.3	0.3	0.3	1.4
Tax incentives for preserving historic structures	0.3	0.4	0.4	0.4	0.4	1.8
Expensing costs of removing architectural barriers	0.0	0.0	0.0	0.0	0.0	0.0
CAPITAL GAINS (EXCEPT HOMES)	**66.8**	**69.8**	**72.6**	**75.3**	**79.6**	**364.1**
Exclusion of capital gains on inherited property	25.4	26.7	28.1	29.4	31.9	141.6
Lower rates on capital gains income	38.7	40.2	41.4	42.7	44.2	207.2
Deferral on "like-kind exchanges"	1.4	1.5	1.6	1.6	1.7	7.8
Carryover basis of capital gains on gifts	1.2	1.3	1.5	1.6	1.8	7.4

APPENDIX 2 CONTINUED
TAX EXPENDITURES, FISCAL 2000–2004, DETAILED LIST
($ BILLIONS)

	Corporations and Individuals Combined					
	2000	2001	2002	2003	2004	2000–2004
Deferral of gain in disaster areas	0.0	0.0	0.0	0.0	0.0	0.1
TAX-FREE BONDS, PUBLIC (WITH STATE AND LOCAL SAVINGS)	**23.0**	**23.2**	**23.4**	**23.7**	**23.9**	**117.2**
TAX-FREE BONDS, PRIVATE (WITH NONPROFIT SAVINGS)	**4.8**	**4.9**	**4.9**	**5.0**	**5.1**	**24.7**
Mortgage subsidy bonds	0.9	0.9	0.9	0.9	1.0	4.7
Private, nonprofit health facility bonds	1.2	1.2	1.3	1.3	1.3	6.3
Airports, docks, sports and convention facilities bonds	0.7	0.7	0.8	0.8	0.8	3.7
Rental housing bonds	0.2	0.2	0.2	0.2	0.2	0.8
Private, nonprofit educational facility bonds	0.6	0.6	0.6	0.6	0.6	3.0
Pollution control, sewage & waste disposal facilities	0.5	0.5	0.5	0.5	0.5	2.4
Small-issue industrial development bonds	0.3	0.3	0.3	0.3	0.3	1.6
Energy facility bonds	0.1	0.1	0.1	0.1	0.1	0.6
Credit for holders of zone academy bonds	0.0	0.0	0.0	0.1	0.1	0.2
Credit for holders of zone academy bonds	0.0	0.0	0.0	0.1	0.1	0.2
Student loan bonds	0.3	0.3	0.3	0.3	0.3	1.3
Veterans housing bonds	0.0	0.0	0.0	0.0	0.0	0.2
INSURANCE COMPANIES AND PRODUCTS	**28.6**	**29.5**	**30.3**	**31.3**	**32.4**	**152.1**
Exclusion of interest on life insurance savings	24.2	24.9	25.7	26.5	27.4	128.7

Appendix 2 Continued
Tax Expenditures, Fiscal 2000–2004, Detailed List
($ Billions)

	Corporations and Individuals Combined					
	2000	2001	2002	2003	2004	2000–2004
Special treatment of life insurance company reserves	1.1	1.2	1.2	1.3	1.3	6.1
Deduction of unpaid loss reserves for property and causality companies	2.8	2.9	2.9	3.0	3.1	14.7
Special deduction for Blue Cross/Blue Shield companies	0.2	0.2	0.1	0.1	0.2	0.8
Exemption for insurance companies owned by tax-exempt organizations	0.2	0.2	0.2	0.3	0.3	1.2
Small life insurance company deduction	0.1	0.1	0.1	0.1	0.1	0.5
Special alternative tax on small P and C insurance companies	0.0	0.0	0.0	0.0	0.0	0.0
MULTINATIONAL TAX BREAKS	**19.1**	**20.5**	**20.7**	**21.1**	**22.2**	**103.6**
Inventory property sales source rules exception	4.0	4.2	4.4	4.6	4.8	22.0
Possessions tax credit	3.2	3.3	3.1	2.9	2.8	15.3
Exclusion of income earned abroad by U.S. citizens	2.9	3.1	3.4	3.7	4.0	17.1
Deferral of income from controlled foreign corporations	4.8	5.2	5.5	5.8	6.2	27.5
Exclusion of income of Foreign Sales Corporations	3.3	3.5	3.8	4.0	4.4	19.0
Interest allocation rules for certain financial options	0.8	1.1	0.5	—	—	2.4
Deferral of tax on shipping companies	0.1	0.1	0.1	0.1	0.1	0.3
BUSINESS MEALS AND ENTERTAINMENT*	**6.6**	**6.9**	**7.2**	**7.5**	**7.8**	**36.0**

* Business meals and entertainment are not in the Treasury Department or Joint Committee on Taxation tables.

Appendix 2 Continued
Tax Expenditures, Fiscal 2000–2004, Detailed List
($ Billions)

	Corporations and Individuals Combined					
	2000	2001	2002	2003	2004	2000–2004
Oil, Gas, Energy	**3.1**	**3.2**	**3.3**	**3.1**	**3.1**	**15.9**
Alternative fuel production credit	1.1	1.1	1.2	0.8	0.8	5.1
Oil, gas and other fuels percentage depletion	0.7	0.7	0.7	0.7	0.7	3.3
Gasoline, excise tax exemption and credit	0.6	0.6	0.7	0.7	0.7	3.3
New technology credit	0.1	0.1	0.1	0.1	0.1	0.6
Exclusion of conservation subsidies from utilities	0.1	0.1	0.1	0.1	0.1	0.3
Expensing of intang. drilling costs	0.2	0.2	0.3	0.3	0.3	1.2
Enhanced oil recovery costs credit	0.2	0.2	0.2	0.2	0.3	1.0
Tax breaks for "clean-fuel" vehicles & properties	0.1	0.1	0.1	0.1	0.1	0.4
Special tax rate for nuke decom. reserve fund	0.1	0.1	0.1	0.2	0.2	0.8
Low-income Housing Credit	**3.4**	**3.6**	**3.7**	**3.8**	**3.8**	**18.2**
R&E Tax Breaks	**2.9**	**5.5**	**7.7**	**5.9**	**5.9**	**27.9**
Expensing of research expenditures	2.4	2.4	2.4	2.6	2.7	12.5
Credit for increasing research activities	0.5	3.2	5.3	3.3	3.2	15.5
Timber, Agriculture, Minerals	**1.5**	**1.8**	**1.7**	**1.8**	**1.8**	**8.6**
Expensing of multiperiod timber growing costs	0.3	0.4	0.4	0.4	0.4	1.8
Percentage depletion, nonfuel minerals	0.3	0.3	0.3	0.3	0.3	1.4

APPENDIX 2 CONTINUED
TAX EXPENDITURES, FISCAL 2000–2004, DETAILED LIST
($ BILLIONS)

	Corporations and Individuals Combined					
	2000	2001	2002	2003	2004	2000–2004
Expensing of certain multiperiod agriculture costs	0.1	0.2	0.2	0.2	0.2	0.9
Cash accounting for agriculture	0.5	0.6	0.6	0.6	0.6	3.0
Expensing of soil & water conservation expenses	0.1	0.1	0.1	0.1	0.1	0.3
Special rules for mining reclamation reserves	0.0	0.0	0.0	0.0	0.0	0.2
Expensing of exploration costs, nonfuel minerals	0.0	0.1	0.1	0.1	0.1	0.2
Reforestation tax breaks	0.0	0.0	0.0	0.0	0.0	0.1
Solvent farmers treated as bankrupt on loans	0.0	0.0	0.0	0.0	0.0	0.1
Exclusion of cost-sharing payments	0.0	0.0	0.0	0.0	0.0	0.1
5-year carryback period for farming NOLs	0.1	0.1	0.0	0.0	0.0	0.3
Income averaging for farmers	0.0	0.0	0.0	0.0	0.0	0.2
Deferral of gain on sale of farm refiners	0.0	0.0	0.0	0.0	0.0	0.1
SPECIAL ESOP RULES	**1.1**	**1.1**	**1.1**	**1.2**	**1.3**	**5.8**
FINANCIAL INSTITUTIONS (NON-INSURANCE)	**1.2**	**1.3**	**1.4**	**1.4**	**1.5**	**6.9**
Exemption of credit union income	1.2	1.3	1.3	1.4	1.5	6.7
Excess bad debt reserves of financial institutions	0.1	0.1	0.0	0.0	0.0	0.2
INSTALLMENT SALES	**0.8**	**0.8**	**0.8**	**0.8**	**0.8**	**3.9**
EMPOWERMENT ZONES	**0.4**	**0.5**	**0.5**	**0.4**	**0.3**	**2.0**

Appendix 2 Continued
Tax Expenditures, Fiscal 2000–2004, Detailed List
($ Billions)

	Corporations and Individuals Combined					
	2000	2001	2002	2003	2004	2000–2004
Other business and investment	**12.0**	**12.2**	**12.6**	**12.7**	**13.2**	**62.6**
Graduated corporate income tax rates	5.3	5.2	5.4	5.5	5.7	27.1
Corporate charitable deductions	3.2	3.4	3.7	4.0	4.4	18.7
Deferral of interest on savings bonds	1.1	1.2	1.2	1.2	1.2	5.9
Exclusion from NOL limits for bankrupt corporations	0.5	0.5	0.5	0.5	0.5	2.5
Completed contract rules	0.2	0.2	0.2	0.2	0.2	1.1
Permanent exceptions from imputed interest rules	0.2	0.2	0.2	0.2	0.2	1.0
Cancellation of indebtedness	0.0	0.0	0.0	0.0	0.0	0.1
Cash accounting other than agriculture	0.1	0.1	0.1	0.1	0.1	0.6
Credit for disabled access expenditures	0.1	0.1	0.1	0.1	0.1	0.4
Investment credit for fixing up structures	0.0	0.0	0.0	0.0	0.0	0.1
Exemption of certain mutuals' and corporation income	0.1	0.1	0.1	0.1	0.1	0.3
Work opportunity tax credit	0.5	0.4	0.3	0.2	0.1	1.5
Welfare-to-work tax credit	0.1	0.1	0.1	0.0	0.1	0.3
Expensing of magazine circulation expenditures	0.0	0.0	0.0	0.0	0.0	0.2
Special rules for magazine, book, and record returns	0.0	0.0	0.0	0.0	0.0	0.1

Appendix 2 Continued
Tax Expenditures, Fiscal 2000–2004, Detailed List
($ Billions)

	2000	2001	2002	2003	2004	2000–2004
				Corporations and Individuals Combined		
Exclusion of contrib. to construct. of water and sewer utilities	0.0	0.0	0.0	0.0	0.0	0.1
Tax credit for employer-paid FICA taxes on tips	0.3	0.3	0.4	0.4	0.4	1.8
Expensing redev. costs in contaminated areas	0.1	0.1	0.1	–0.0	–0.0	0.3
Tax credit for orphan drug research	0.1	0.1	0.1	0.1	0.1	0.5
Subtotal, Business and Investment	**214.3**	**225.8**	**232.7**	**235.4**	**243.7**	**1,151.9**
Pensions, Keoghs, IRAs	**101.3**	**106.4**	**111.6**	**117.0**	**122.3**	**558.5**
Employer pension plans	82.4	86.5	90.3	94.5	98.7	452.5
Individual Retirement Accounts	13.6	14.3	15.5	16.5	17.4	77.3
Keogh self-employed plans	5.3	5.5	5.7	6.0	6.2	28.7
Other savings	**0.2**	**0.2**	**0.2**	**0.3**	**0.3**	**1.3**
Education IRAs and State tuition plan deferrals	0.2	0.2	0.2	0.3	0.3	1.2
Medical Savings Accounts	0.0	0.0	0.0	0.0	0.0	0.1
Subtotal, Retirement and Other Savings	**101.5**	**106.6**	**111.8**	**117.3**	**122.6**	**559.8**

Appendix 2 Continued
Tax Expenditures, Fiscal 2000–2004, Detailed List
($ Billions)

	Corporations					
	2000	2001	2002	2003	2004	2000–2004
TOTAL CORPORATIONS	**81.2**	**88.1**	**91.1**	**89.9**	**92.5**	**442.8**
ACCELERATED DEPRECIATION	**25.8**	**27.8**	**27.7**	**27.7**	**28.2**	**137.1**
Accelerated depreciation of machinery and equipment	23.5	25.6	25.5	25.6	26.3	126.6
Accelerated depreciation of buildings except rental housing	1.5	1.2	1.2	1.1	0.9	5.9
Accelerated depreciation on rental housing	0.2	0.2	0.2	0.2	0.2	0.9
Expensing of certain small equipment investments	0.3	0.4	0.4	0.4	0.4	1.9
Amortization of business start-up costs	0.1	0.1	0.1	0.1	0.1	0.3
Tax incentives for preservation of historic structures	0.2	0.3	0.3	0.3	0.3	1.4
Expensing of costs of removing architectural barriers	—	0.0	0.0	0.0	0.0	0.0
MULTINATIONAL TAX BREAKS	**16.2**	**17.4**	**17.3**	**17.4**	**18.2**	**86.5**
Inventory property sales source rules exception	4.0	4.2	4.4	4.6	4.8	22.0
Possessions tax credit	3.2	3.3	3.1	2.9	2.8	15.3
Deferral of income from controlled foreign corporations	4.8	5.2	5.5	5.8	6.2	27.5
Exclusion of income of Foreign Sales Corporations	3.3	3.5	3.8	4.0	4.4	19.0
Interest allocation rules exception for certain financial ops.	0.8	1.1	0.5	—	—	2.4
Deferral of tax on shipping companies	0.1	0.1	0.1	0.1	0.1	0.3
INSURANCE COMPANIES AND PRODUCTS	**5.7**	**5.9**	**6.0**	**6.2**	**6.5**	**30.3**
Special treatment of life insurance company reserves	1.1	1.2	1.2	1.3	1.3	6.1

Appendix 2 Continued
Tax Expenditures, Fiscal 2000–2004, Detailed List
($ Billions)

	Corporations					
	2000	2001	2002	2003	2004	2000–2004
Deduction of unpaid loss reserves for P and C companies	2.8	2.9	2.9	3.0	3.1	14.7
Exclusion of interest on life insurance savings	1.3	1.3	1.4	1.4	1.5	6.9
Special deduction for Blue Cross/Blue Shield companies	0.2	0.2	0.1	0.1	0.2	0.8
Exemption for ins. comps. owned by tax-exempt orgs.	0.2	0.2	0.2	0.3	0.3	1.2
Small life insurance company deduction	0.1	0.1	0.1	0.1	0.1	0.5
Special alternative tax on small property and casualty ins. cos.	0.0	0.0	0.0	0.0	0.0	0.0
TAX-FREE BONDS, PUBLIC (EXCLUDES STATE AND LOCAL SAVINGS)	**5.8**	**5.9**	**5.9**	**6.0**	**6.0**	**29.5**
TAX-FREE BONDS, PRIVATE (EXCLUDES NONPROFIT SAVINGS)	**2.1**	**2.2**	**2.2**	**2.2**	**2.2**	**10.9**
Airports, docks, and sports and convention facilities bonds	0.4	0.4	0.4	0.4	0.4	2.2
Pollution control and sewage and waste disposal facilities	0.3	0.3	0.3	0.3	0.3	1.4
Small-issue industrial development bonds	0.2	0.2	0.2	0.2	0.2	0.9
Energy facility bonds	0.1	0.1	0.1	0.1	0.1	0.3
Private, nonprofit health facility bonds	0.3	0.3	0.3	0.3	0.3	1.6
Mortgage subsidy bonds	0.2	0.2	0.2	0.2	0.2	1.2
Rental housing bonds	0.1	0.1	0.1	0.1	0.1	0.6
Private, nonprofit educational facility bonds	0.4	0.5	0.5	0.5	0.5	2.3
Credit for holders of zone academy bonds	0.0	0.0	0.0	0.0	0.1	0.2
Student loan bonds	0.1	0.1	0.1	0.1	0.1	0.3
Veterans housing bonds	0.0	0.0	0.0	0.0	0.0	0.0

Appendix 2 Continued
Tax Expenditures, Fiscal 2000–2004, Detailed List
($ billions)

	Corporations					
	2000	2001	2002	2003	2004	2000–2004
Business meals and entertainment*	**4.1**	**4.3**	**4.5**	**4.7**	**4.9**	**22.5**
R&E tax breaks	**2.8**	**5.5**	**7.6**	**5.9**	**5.9**	**27.7**
Expensing of research and experimentation expenditures	2.4	2.3	2.4	2.6	2.7	12.3
Credit for increasing research activities	0.5	3.2	5.2	3.3	3.2	15.4
Oil, gas, energy	**2.7**	**2.7**	**2.8**	**2.6**	**2.6**	**13.4**
Alternative fuel production credit	1.0	1.0	1.0	0.7	0.7	4.3
Gasohol, excise tax exemption and credit	0.6	0.6	0.7	0.7	0.7	3.2
Oil, gas, and other fuels, percentage depletion	0.5	0.5	0.5	0.5	0.5	2.3
New technology credit	0.0	0.0	0.1	0.1	0.1	0.2
Oil, gas, and other fuels, expensing of intangible drilling costs	0.2	0.2	0.3	0.3	0.3	1.2
Exclusion of conservation subsidies provided by utilities	-0.0	-0.0	-0.0	—	—	-0.0
Tax credit & deduction for "clean-fuel" vehicles and properties	0.1	0.1	0.1	0.1	0.0	0.4
Enhanced oil recovery costs credit	0.1	0.2	0.2	0.2	0.2	1.0
Special tax rate for nuclear decommissioning reserve fund	0.1	0.1	0.1	0.2	0.2	0.8
Special ESOP rules	**0.8**	**0.9**	**0.9**	**0.9**	**1.0**	**4.5**
Financial institutions (noninsurance)	1.2	1.3	1.4	1.4	1.5	6.9
Exemption of credit union income	1.2	1.3	1.3	1.4	1.5	6.7
Excess bad debt reserves of financial institutions	0.1	0.1	0.0	0.0	0.0	0.2

* Business meals and entertainment are not in the Treasury Department or Joint Committee on Taxation tables.

APPENDIX 2 CONTINUED
TAX EXPENDITURES, FISCAL 2000–2004, DETAILED LIST
($ BILLIONS)

	Corporations					
	2000	2001	2002	2003	2004	2000–2004
LOW-INCOME HOUSING CREDIT	**1.8**	**1.9**	**1.9**	**2.0**	**2.0**	**9.6**
TIMBER, AGRICULTURE, MINERALS	**0.5**	**0.6**	**0.6**	**0.6**	**0.6**	**2.9**
Expensing of multiperiod timber growing costs	0.2	0.3	0.3	0.3	0.3	1.3
Percentage depletion, nonfuel minerals	0.2	0.2	0.2	0.2	0.2	1.0
Expensing of certain multiperiod agriculture costs	0.0	0.0	0.0	0.0	0.0	0.0
Cash accounting for agriculture	0.0	0.0	0.0	0.0	0.0	0.1
Special rules for mining reclamation reserves	0.0	0.0	0.0	0.0	0.0	0.1
Expensing exploration and development costs, nonfuel minerals	0.0	0.1	0.1	0.1	0.1	0.2
Expensing of soil and water conservation expenditures	0.0	0.0	0.0	0.0	0.0	0.1
Exclusion of cost-sharing payments	0.0	0.0	0.0	0.0	0.0	0.1
Five-year carryback period for NOLs attributable to farming	0.0	0.0	0.0	0.0	0.0	0.1
CAPITAL GAINS (EXCEPT HOMES)	**1.0**	**1.1**	**1.2**	**1.2**	**1.3**	**5.8**
Deferral on "like-kind exchanges"	1.0	1.1	1.2	1.2	1.3	5.8
INSTALLMENT SALES	**0.2**	**0.2**	**0.2**	**0.2**	**0.2**	**1.2**
EMPOWERMENT ZONES	**0.2**	**0.2**	**0.2**	**0.2**	**0.2**	**1.1**
OTHER BUSINESS AND INVESTMENT	**10.1**	**10.3**	**10.6**	**10.7**	**11.2**	**53.0**
Graduated corporate income tax rates	5.3	5.2	5.4	5.5	5.7	27.1

Appendix 2 Continued
Tax Expenditures, Fiscal 2000–2004, Detailed List
($ Billions)

	Corporations					
	2000	2001	2002	2003	2004	2000–2004
Corporate charitable deductions	3.2	3.4	3.7	4.0	4.4	18.7
Exclusion from net operating loss limits for bankrupt corps.	0.5	0.5	0.5	0.5	0.5	2.5
Completed contract rules	0.2	0.2	0.2	0.2	0.2	1.0
Credit for disabled access expenditures	0.0	0.0	0.0	0.0	0.0	0.0
Exemption of certain mutuals' and cooperatives' income	0.1	0.1	0.1	0.1	0.1	0.3
Work opportunity tax credit	0.4	0.4	0.3	0.1	0.1	1.3
Welfare-to-work tax credit	0.1	0.1	0.1	0.0	0.0	0.3
Investment credit for fixing up structures (nonhistoric)	0.0	0.0	0.0	0.0	0.0	0.1
Cash accounting other than agriculture	0.0	0.0	0.0	0.0	0.0	0.1
Expensing of magazine circulation expenditures	0.0	0.0	0.0	0.0	0.0	0.1
Permanent exceptions from imputed interest rules	0.0	0.0	0.0	0.0	0.0	0.0
Special rules for magazine, book, and record returns	0.0	0.0	0.0	0.0	0.0	0.1
Exclusion of contribution to construct utilities	0.0	0.0	0.0	0.0	0.0	0.1
Tax credit for employer-paid FICA taxes on tips	0.1	0.1	0.1	0.1	0.1	0.6
Expensing redevelopment costs in contaminated areas	0.1	0.1	0.1	-0.0	-0.0	0.2
Tax credit for orphan drug research	0.1	0.1	0.1	0.1	0.1	0.5

Appendix 2 Continued
Tax Expenditures, Fiscal 2000–2004, Detailed List
($ billions)

	Corporations and Individuals Combined					
	2000	2001	2002	2003	2004	2000–2004
TOTAL INDIVIDUALS	**541.0**	**563.8**	**586.9**	**611.8**	**637.6**	**2,941.1**
Individual Tax Expenditures for Business, Savings, and Investment						
CAPITAL GAINS (EXCEPT HOMES)	**65.8**	**68.7**	**71.4**	**74.1**	**78.3**	**358.3**
Exclusion of capital gains on inherited property	25.4	26.7	28.1	29.4	31.9	141.6
Lower rates on capital gains income	38.7	40.2	41.4	42.7	44.2	207.2
Carryover basis of capital gains on gifts	1.2	1.3	1.5	1.6	1.8	7.4
Deferral on "like-kind exchanges"	0.4	0.4	0.4	0.4	0.4	2.0
Deferral of gain in disaster areas	0.0	0.0	0.0	0.0	0.0	0.1
INSURANCE PRODUCTS	**22.9**	**23.6**	**24.3**	**25.1**	**25.9**	**121.8**
Exclusion of interest on life insurance savings	22.9	23.6	24.3	25.1	25.9	121.8
ACCELERATED DEPRECIATION	**13.2**	**13.2**	**13.2**	**13.0**	**12.8**	**65.3**
Accelerated depreciation of machinery	6.2	6.2	6.1	6.1	6.1	30.8
Accelerated depreciation on rental housing	5.2	5.2	5.2	5.3	5.4	26.3
Accelerated dep. of buildings (without rental housing)	0.7	0.5	0.5	0.4	0.3	2.4
Expensing of small equipment investments	0.8	0.9	1.0	0.8	0.7	4.3
Amortization of business start-up costs	0.2	0.2	0.2	0.2	0.2	1.1

Appendix 2 Continued
Tax Expenditures, Fiscal 2000–2004, Detailed List
($ billions)

	Corporations and Individuals Combined					
	2000	2001	2002	2003	2004	2000–2004
Tax incentives for preserving historic structures	0.1	0.1	0.1	0.1	0.1	0.4
Expensing for removing architectural barriers	0.0	0.0	—	—	—	0.0
TAX-FREE BONDS, PUBLIC (EXCLUDES SAVINGS AND LOAN SAVINGS)	**9.2**	**9.3**	**9.4**	**9.5**	**9.6**	**46.9**
TAX-FREE BONDS, PRIVATE (EXCLUDES NONPROFITS)	**2.2**	**2.2**	**2.2**	**2.2**	**2.2**	**11.0**
Mortgage subsidy bonds	0.7	0.7	0.7	0.7	0.7	3.5
Rental housing bonds	0.0	0.0	0.0	0.0	0.0	0.2
Private nonprofit health facility bonds	0.5	0.5	0.5	0.5	0.5	2.5
Student loan bonds	0.2	0.2	0.2	0.2	0.2	1.0
Airports, docks, sports and convention facilities	0.3	0.3	0.3	0.3	0.3	1.5
Private, nonprofit educational facility bonds	0.1	0.1	0.1	0.1	0.1	0.4
Pollution control, sewage and waste disposal	0.2	0.2	0.2	0.2	0.2	0.9
Small-issue industrial development bonds	0.1	0.1	0.1	0.1	0.1	0.6
Veterans housing bonds	0.0	0.0	0.0	0.0	0.0	0.2
Energy facility bonds	0.0	0.0	0.0	0.0	0.0	0.2
MULTINATIONAL TAX BREAKS	**2.9**	**3.1**	**3.4**	**3.7**	**4.0**	**17.1**
Exclusion of income abroad by U.S. citizens	2.9	3.1	3.4	3.7	4.0	17.1
Business meals & entertainment*	2.5	2.6	2.7	2.8	2.9	13.5
Low-income housing credit	1.6	1.7	1.7	1.8	1.8	8.6

* Business meals and entertainment are not in the Treasury Department or Joint Committee on Taxation tables.

Appendix 2 Continued
Tax Expenditures, Fiscal 2000–2004, Detailed List
($ Billions)

	Corporations and Individuals Combined					
	2000	2001	2002	2003	2004	2000–2004
TIMBER, AGRICULTURE, MINERALS	**1.0**	**1.2**	**1.1**	**1.2**	**1.2**	**5.7**
Expensing of multiperiod timber growing costs	0.1	0.1	0.1	0.1	0.1	0.5
Cash accounting for agriculture	0.5	0.6	0.6	0.6	0.6	2.9
Expensing of multiperiod agriculture costs	0.1	0.2	0.2	0.2	0.2	0.8
Percentage depletion, nonfuel minerals	0.1	0.1	0.1	0.1	0.1	0.4
Expensing of soil & water conservation costs	0.0	0.0	0.0	0.0	0.0	0.2
Loans forgiven solvent farmers as if bankrupt	0.0	0.0	0.0	0.0	0.0	0.1
Credit and 7-year amortization for reforestation	0.0	0.0	0.0	0.0	0.0	0.1
Exclusion of cost-sharing payments	0.0	0.0	0.0	0.0	0.0	0.1
Expensing of exploration costs, nonfuel minerals	0.0	0.0	0.0	0.0	0.0	0.0
Special rules for mining reclamation reserves	0.0	0.0	0.0	0.0	0.0	0.1
Income averaging for farmers	0.0	0.0	0.0	0.0	0.0	0.2
Five-year carryback for NOLs for farming	0.1	0.1	0.0	0.0	0.0	0.3
Deferral of gain on sale of farm refiners	0.0	0.0	0.0	0.0	0.0	0.1
INSTALLMENT SALES	**0.5**	**0.5**	**0.5**	**0.5**	**0.6**	**2.7**
OIL, GAS, ENERGY	**0.5**	**0.5**	**0.5**	**0.5**	**0.5**	**2.5**
Oil, gas and other fuels, percentage depletion	0.2	0.2	0.2	0.2	0.2	0.9
Alternative fuel production credit	0.1	0.2	0.2	0.2	0.2	0.8
Exclusion of conservation subsidies from utilities	0.1	0.1	0.1	0.1	0.1	0.3

Appendix 2 Continued
Tax Expenditures, Fiscal 2000–2004, Detailed List
($ Billions)

	Corporations and Individuals Combined					
	2000	2001	2002	2003	2004	2000–2004
Oil, gas, and other fuels expensing of intangible drilling costs	0.0	0.0	0.0	0.0	0.0	0.0
Tax credit & deduction for "clean-fuel"	0.0	0.0	0.0	0.0	0.0	0.1
New technology credit	0.1	0.1	0.1	0.1	0.1	0.3
Enhanced oil recovery costs credit	0.0	0.0	0.0	0.0	0.0	0.1
Gasohol, excise tax exemption and credit	0.0	0.0	0.0	0.0	0.0	0.0
Empowerment zones	**0.2**	**0.2**	**0.2**	**0.2**	**0.2**	**1.0**
R and E tax breaks	**0.0**	**0.1**	**0.1**	**0.0**	**0.0**	**0.3**
Expensing of research and experimentation costs	0.0	0.0	0.0	0.0	0.0	0.1
Credit for increasing research activities	0.0	0.0	0.0	0.0	0.0	0.1
Deferral of interest on savings bonds	1.1	1.2	1.2	1.2	1.2	5.9
Exceptions to imputed interest rules	0.2	0.2	0.2	0.2	0.2	1.0
Cash accounting other than agriculture	0.1	0.1	0.1	0.1	0.1	0.5
Credit for fixing up structures (nonhistoric)	0.0	0.0	0.0	0.0	0.0	0.1
Expensing of magazine circulation costs	0.0	0.0	0.0	0.0	0.0	0.1
Credit for disabled access expenditures	0.1	0.1	0.1	0.1	0.1	0.3
Cancellation of indebtedness	0.0	0.0	0.0	0.0	0.0	0.1
Completed contract rules	0.0	0.0	0.0	0.0	0.0	0.1
Work opportunity tax credit	0.1	0.1	0.1	0.0	0.0	0.2

APPENDIX 2 CONTINUED
TAX EXPENDITURES, FISCAL 2000–2004, DETAILED LIST
($ BILLIONS)

	Corporations and Individuals Combined					
	2000	2001	2002	2003	2004	2000–2004
Welfare-to-work tax credit	0.0	0.0	0.0	0.0	0.0	0.1
Tax credit for employer-paid FICA taxes on tips	0.2	0.2	0.2	0.2	0.2	1.2
Expensing redev. costs in contaminated areas	0.0	0.0	0.0	0.0	0.0	0.1
Special rules for magazine, book, and record returns	0.0	0.0	0.0	0.0	0.0	0.1
SUBTOTAL, BUSINESS AND INVESTMENT	**124.6**	**129.1**	**133.0**	**136.7**	**142.3**	**665.6**
PENSIONS, KEOGHS, IRAs	**101.3**	**106.4**	**111.6**	**117.0**	**122.3**	**558.5**
Employer pension plans	82.4	86.5	90.3	94.5	98.7	452.5
Individual Retirement Accounts	13.6	14.3	15.5	16.5	17.4	77.3
Keogh self-employed plans	5.3	5.5	5.7	6.0	6.2	28.7
OTHER SAVINGS	**0.2**	**0.2**	**0.2**	**0.3**	**0.3**	**1.3**
Education IRAs and State tuition plan deferrals	0.2	0.2	0.2	0.3	0.3	1.2
Medical Savings Accounts	0.0	0.0	0.0	0.0	0.0	0.1
TOTAL, BUSINESS, INVESTMENT, AND SAVINGS	**226.1**	**235.7**	**244.8**	**254.0**	**264.9**	**1,225.4**

APPENDIX 2 CONTINUED
TAX EXPENDITURES, FISCAL 2000–2004, DETAILED LIST
($ BILLIONS)

	Individuals					
	2000	2001	2002	2003	2004	2000–2004
INDIVIDUAL TAX EXPENDITURES FOR PERSONAL ACTIVITIES						
ITEMIZED DEDUCTIONS	**111.6**	**116.8**	**122.2**	**127.9**	**133.9**	**612.5**
OTHER FRINGE BENEFIT EXCLUSIONS	**15.8**	**16.6**	**17.3**	**18.1**	**18.9**	**86.7**
Miscellaneous fringe benefits	6.5	6.9	7.3	7.8	8.2	36.7
Group term life insurance	1.9	1.9	2.0	2.1	2.2	10.1
Employer-paid transportation benefits	2.8	2.8	2.9	3.0	3.1	14.7
Cafeteria plan fringe benefits (nonhealth)	1.7	1.8	2.0	2.1	2.3	9.9
Employer-provided child care	0.5	0.6	0.6	0.6	0.7	3.0
Employee meals and lodging (nonmilitary)	0.7	0.8	0.8	0.8	0.9	4.0
Parsonage allowances	0.4	0.4	0.4	0.4	0.4	2.0
Voluntary employee benefits assn. benefits	0.7	0.8	0.8	0.9	0.9	4.0
Accident and disability insurance	0.2	0.2	0.2	0.2	0.2	1.0
Employee awards	0.1	0.1	0.1	0.1	0.1	0.7
Employer education assistance	0.3	0.3	0.1	—	—	0.7
EARNED INCOME TAX CREDIT	**30.1**	**30.4**	**31.5**	**32.3**	**33.3**	**157.7**
Earned income tax credit, refundable part	25.7	26.0	26.9	27.5	28.4	134.6
Earned income credit, nonrefundable part	4.4	4.4	4.5	4.8	4.9	23.1
SOCIAL SECURITY BENEFITS (EXCLUSION)	**24.7**	**25.8**	**27.1**	**28.4**	**29.7**	**135.6**

APPENDIX 2 CONTINUED
TAX EXPENDITURES, FISCAL 2000–2004, DETAILED LIST
($ BILLIONS)

	Individuals					
	2000	2001	2002	2003	2004	2000–2004
CHILD CREDIT	**19.0**	**19.0**	**18.6**	**18.2**	**17.6**	**92.4**
CAPITAL GAINS ON HOMES	**15.7**	**16.0**	**16.3**	**16.7**	**17.0**	**81.8**
WORKMEN'S COMPENSATION, ETC.	**10.3**	**10.8**	**11.3**	**11.8**	**12.3**	**56.6**
Workmen's compensation benefits	9.7	10.2	10.7	11.2	11.6	53.4
Public assistance benefits	0.5	0.5	0.5	0.6	0.6	2.8
Special benefits for disabled coal miners	0.1	0.1	0.1	0.1	0.1	0.4
EDUCATION CREDITS AND DEDUCTIONS	**7.6**	**7.9**	**8.0**	**9.5**	**9.4**	**42.4**
HOPE tax credit	4.9	5.1	5.1	4.7	4.6	24.6
Lifetime Learning tax credit	2.4	2.4	2.5	4.4	4.4	16.1
Deductibility of student loan interest	0.3	0.3	0.4	0.4	0.4	1.8
SOLDIERS AND VETERANS EXCLUSIONS	**4.9**	**5.0**	**5.2**	**5.4**	**5.5**	**26.0**
Benefits and allowances to soldiers	2.1	2.0	2.1	2.1	2.1	10.4
Veterans disability compensation	2.6	2.7	2.8	2.9	3.0	14.1
Military disability benefits	0.1	0.1	0.1	0.1	0.1	0.6
GI bill benefits	0.1	0.1	0.1	0.1	0.1	0.5
Veterans' pensions	0.1	0.1	0.1	0.1	0.1	0.5
CHILD AND DEPENDENT CARE CREDIT	**2.3**	**2.3**	**2.3**	**2.3**	**2.2**	**11.3**

APPENDIX 2 CONTINUED
TAX EXPENDITURES, FISCAL 2000–2004, DETAILED LIST
($ BILLIONS)

	Individuals					
	2000	2001	2002	2003	2004	2000–2004
ELDERLY AND BLIND	**2.0**	**2.0**	**2.1**	**2.1**	**2.2**	**10.4**
Increased std. deduction for blind and elderly	1.9	2.0	2.1	2.1	2.2	10.3
Tax credit for low-income elderly and disabled	0.0	0.0	0.0	0.0	0.0	0.1
OTHER PERSONAL	**3.6**	**3.9**	**4.2**	**4.9**	**5.5**	**22.0**
Exclusion of scholarships and fellowships	1.1	1.2	1.2	1.3	1.3	6.1
Parental personal exemption for students age 19+	0.8	0.9	0.9	1.0	1.0	4.6
Deduction for self-employed health insurance	1.2	1.3	1.6	2.2	2.9	9.2
Exclusion of certain foster care payments	0.3	0.3	0.3	0.3	0.3	1.5
Exclusion of savings bond interest for education	0.0	0.0	0.0	0.0	0.0	0.1
Adoption credit and exclusion	0.2	0.2	0.2	0.1	0.0	0.7
TOTAL, PERSONAL ACTIVITIES	**314.9**	**328.1**	**342.1**	**357.8**	**372.7**	**1,715.7**

Sources: U.S. Congress Joint Committee on Taxation, "Estimates of Federal Tax Expenditures for Fiscal Year 2000-2004," December 22, 1999, Office of Management and Budget, "Tax Expenditures," February 2000, Microsimulation Tax Model, Institute on Taxation and Economic Policy, March 2000, Washington, D.C. Figures are generally averages from the first two sources, except where an item was listed in only one source or one source was based on more current information (or otherwise appeared to be more accurate). Tax-exempt interest benefits were recalculated and reallocated to take account of lower interest rates received by bondholders, benefits to borrowers, and other concerns. A few items, such as business meals and entertainment, are not on either list and were calculated by the Insitute on Taxation and Economic Policy. All figures are for fiscal years.

Notes

Chapter 1

1. U.S. Congress, Joint Committee on Taxation, "Estimates of Federal Tax Expenditures for Fiscal Years 2000–2004," December 22, 1999, p. 2. See also Congressional Budget and Impoundment Control Act of 1974 (P.L. 93–344), sec. 3(a)(3).

2. Office of Management and Budget, "Tax Expenditures," *Budget of the United States Government, Fiscal Year 2001*, Analytical Perspectives, February 2000; U.S. Congress, Joint Committee on Taxation, "Estimates of Federal Tax Expenditures for Fiscal Years 2000–2004."

3. In 1984, the Treasury contended that (a) homeowner property taxes provide direct, measurable benefits to families who pay them, such as better schools, trash collection, etc.; (b) families living in areas with low property taxes get fewer of these services or must purchase them privately; and therefore (c) fairness dictates that property taxes should not be deductible. U.S. Department of the Treasury, Tax Reform for Fairness, Simplicity, and Economic Growth, 1984.

4. A detailed description of the institute's Microsimulation Tax Model can be found at http://www.itepnet.org.

5. Although $50 million is "deminimis" with respect to the scale of the federal budget, it bears noting that taxpayers and voters get upset when the government misspends even much smaller amounts and can be very appreciative of a well-targeted $50 million in government spending.

6. See: U.S. Congress, Committee on the Budget, Tax Expenditures: Compendium of Background Materials on Individual Provisions, Committee on the Budget United States Senate, 105th Cong., 24 sess., December 1998, p. 7.

Chapter 2

1. U.S. Congress, Joint Committee on Taxation, "General Explanation of the Tax Reform Act of 1986," May 4, 1987, p. 98.

2. Most notably, in September 1986 Congress approved the Tax Reform Act of 1986, which increased the top capital gains tax rate from 20 to 28 percent, effective January 1, 1987. This caused a rush by investors to cash in capital gains before the 20 percent rate expired.

3. Leonard E. Burman and William C. Randolph, "Measuring Permanent Responses to Capital-Gains Tax Changes in Panel Data," *American Economic Review* 84, no. 4 (September 1994): 794–809.

4. Robert S. McIntyre and Jeff Spinner, *130 Reasons Why We Need Tax Reform*, Citizens for Tax Justice, Washington, D.C., 1986.

5. Quoted in Howard Gleckman, "So You Thought Tax Reform Would Kill Capital Spending, " *Businessweek*, June 27, 1988, p. 31.

6. Annual Reports, General Electric Company, Fairfield, Conn., 1986–92

7. Internal Revenue Service, *Statistics of Income Bulletin*, Winter 1994–95, p. 217; calculations by the Institute on Taxation and Economic Policy, Washington, D.C.

8. Annual report, Armonk, IBM, N.Y., 1987.

9. Intel Corp. v. Commissioner, 100 T.C. 616 (1993), aff'd. 67 F.3d 1445 (9th Cir. 1995).

10. Congressional Budget Office, *The Shortfall in Corporate Tax Receipts Since the Tax Reform Act of 1986*, May 1992.

11. For long-term corporate bonds, the 7.3 percent rate is net of state income taxes on pretax interest of 7.8 percent. Interest on federal bonds, at 6.5 percent on ten-year-plus bonds, is exempt from state taxes.

12. Such "intangible drilling costs" include wages, the costs of using machinery for grading and drilling, and the cost of unsalvageable materials used in constructing wells. For most businesses, costs such as these would normally be written off over the useful life of the assets created.

13. Technically, gasohol is exempt from 5.4 cents of the 18.4 cents per gallon federal gasoline tax. (There is a corresponding income tax credit for alcohol used as a fuel in applications where the gasoline tax is not assessed, such as farming.) Since the alcohol content of gasohol is 10 percent, the subsidy works out to 54 cents per gallon of alcohol used.

14. Section 262 of the Internal Revenue Code states this principle explicitly.

15. Few personal outlays, most notably mortgage interest, are allowed as itemized deductions in computing individual taxable income. But the mortgage interest deduction is not defended on tax policy grounds as a proper deduction in computing net income (or ability to pay taxes) but rather as a government subsidy for housing. A reasonable case on ability-to-pay grounds can be made for most other itemized deductions, such as state and local taxes, cash charitable giving and extraordinary medical expenses.

16. In some cases, profits on installment sales can be deferred, but the seller must pay interest to the government on the deferred taxes.

17. The official General Explanation of the Tax Reform Act of 1986 noted: "Congress determined that since 1981, the expanded availability of IRAs had no discernible impact on the level of aggregate personal savings" (p. 625).

CHAPTER 3

1. These figures are averages for the first ten years of a thirty-year mortgage at 9 percent annual interest. In later years the subsidy declines because interest falls as a share of total monthly mortgage payments.

2. Some 41 percent of the taxpayers who now itemize mortgage interest would switch to the standard deduction if the mortgage tax break were eliminated, reducing the number of itemizers by 34 percent. In comparison, eliminating deductions for state and local taxes would cut the number of itemizers by 29 percent; wiping out charitable deductions, by 10 percent; and taking away provisions for extraordinary medical expenses, by 4 percent. Thus, the mortgage interest deduction is the single biggest inducement to itemize.

INDEX

About the Authors of the
Background Papers

MICHAEL P. ETTLINGER is deputy director of Public Campaign, a nonprofit organization dedicated to reducing the role of special interest money in American politics. He is lead author of *Who Pays? A Distributional Analysis of the Tax Systems in All 50 States* (Citizens for Tax Justice, 1996). He was formerly tax policy director for Citizens for Tax Justice as well as for the Institute on Taxation and Economic Policy and has served as a legislative counsel with the New York State Assembly.

ERIC TODER is director of the office of research, Internal Revenue Service (IRS) national headquarters. Prior to joining the IRS in 2001, he held a variety of positions in government and private research institutions. Between 1998 and 2001, he was a senior fellow at the Urban Institute, where he conducted and directed research on tax and retirement policy issues. His prior government service includes positions in the U.S. Department of the Treasury, the Congressional Budget Office, the U.S. Department of Energy, and the New Zealand Treasury. From 1993 to 1996 he served as deputy assistant secretary for tax analysis at the U.S. Treasury.

BERNARD WASOW is a senior fellow at The Century Foundation in the Washington, D.C., office. He has been a member of the economics departments at New York University, the University of Nairobi, and the University of British Columbia and a visiting professor at Columbia University, Monash University (Melbourne,

Australia), and the Central European University (Prague, Czechoslovakia). He also has worked in the research department of the Federal Reserve Bank of New York and as a program officer at the Ford Foundation.